Creative Healing

Books by This Author

Creative Clarity (Inspirational Colouring Book)
The Power and Simplicity of Self-Healing
The Spirit Within
Meditation Essentials: How to Quiet Your Mind to Achieve Personal and Professional Success
Soul Food: 101 Inspirational Messages to Nourish and Heal Your Spirit
Soul Food (Vol. 2)
Soul Food (Vol. 3)

Creative Healing

30-Day Workbook and Colouring Journey

Liberty Forrest

Copyright © 2016 Liberty Forrest

All rights reserved. No part of this work may be reproduced or transmit- ted in any form or by any means, electronic or mechanical, including photocopying, recording or any information storage and retrieval system, without permission in writing from the author.

Published by The Creative Cauldron

ISBN-13: 978-0-9879489-0-8

DISCLAIMER

This book is designed to provide information and motivation to its readers. It is sold with the understanding that neither the author nor the publisher is engaged to render any type of psychological, medical, legal, or any other kind of professional advice. Every effort has been taken to ensure that the information contained in this book is accurate and balanced. Conclusions reached have been based on the evidence examined by the author, who has tried to use reliable resources. Information contained herein may become outdated, invalid or subject to debate.

This book is for educational purposes and is designed to provide helpful information only. It is not intended as a substitute for qualified medical or other professional advice, nor should it be used to diagnose or treat any medical condition. Please consult a qualified professionals for advice. If you are considering taking up exercise or changing your diet, lifestyle, or current medications, or do anything that is intended to alter the state of your health, you are advised to consult your doctor or other relevant professionals.

Neither the publisher nor the author shall be liable for any physical, psychological, emotional, financial, or commercial damages, including, but not limited to, special, incidental, consequential or other damages. Readers are responsible for their own choices, actions and results.

This book is dedicated to my dear friends, Sandy Peckinpah and Frank Moffatt

With my love, respect and deepest gratitude xo

Day 1 - Waiting for the Ripples to Reach the Shore...

You might be feeling hurt, angry, powerless, lost, grief, longing, or hopeless. And there could be much more. But the good news is that there is hope. You *can* heal. You can create a happier, more positive and empowered life. And some part of you must believe that or you wouldn't have picked up this book.

Perhaps you feel like you have no control over your situation. Your life blew up and there you stand, holding the charred scraps of it in scorched hands and wondering what on earth to do now. It's bad enough when Life lobs stuff at us that we can fix - even if it's going to take a while. But what do you do when it's something you cannot control?

You wait. You feel powerless. Helpless. It's agonising. But it's all you can do, so you wait.

So where do you begin? You begin where you are, settling into a place of knowing that whatever is going on right now, it's temporary. It's true that the only constant is change; you'll move on from this place but for now, just be still and come to terms with "what is."

The Serenity Prayer could be useful in assisting you now. The entire prayer, by American theologian Reinhold Niebuhr, is longer than the lines that are so well known, but here is the original version of the portion that is relevant for you:

"God, give me grace to accept with serenity the things that cannot be changed, ☐Courage to change the things which should be changed, ☐And the wisdom to distinguish the one from the other."

Begin by considering the aspects of your situation that you cannot change because this is one of the most empowering steps you can take to taking control of your life. As long as you continue to rail against something over which you have no control, you will feel angry, frustrated and powerless.

You can't push a river upstream - or downstream either. Better to put yourself in a raft and float along with the river, just as it is. Conserve your energy and use it for something that you can actually accomplish.

Maybe your life was ticking along just fine, like a little pond, the odd strong wind whipping up waves here and there. But the storms pass and the surface of the water calms as it seeks to find its level, and balance is restored.

And then one day, something tears into your life like a meteorite thundering through the heavens and crashing into that lake, causing an almighty disturbance. The enormous splash creates violent waves that scatter and unsettle everything as they push their way toward the shore.

But soon the shock passes. The traumatic waves subside, naturally seeking their level again, seeking balance as they make their way to the shore, gradually becoming smaller, ever softening, gently rolling, until they are mere ripples dissolving into the sand.

And so it is with the great shocks and disturbances of Life, those events that turn you inside out when you're right smack in the spot where the meteorite comes thundering into your soul. But your Spirit will survive it, even if sometimes, it feels like it won't. Your Spirit will find its level; it will seek balance. Those early difficult moments, slamming into you one after another, intense and frequent like ominous, rolling waves, will gradually dissolve into the gentle ripples of easier days.

And one day, the last little ripple caused by that initial, thunderous shock, will quietly tickle its way onto the sand and balance will once again be restored.

Wherever you are in that lake, whether fighting to keep your head above water in those horrible first waves, or whether you're somewhere along the more gently bobbing ones, just keep your eye on the shore and know that you are a little closer to it today than you were yesterday. Just know that this too shall pass and one way or another, you ***will*** move on from this place. It is inevitable.

Invitation: Today, I invite you to look closely at those few lines of the Serenity Prayer. Take some time to write about them in a way that is positive and forward-thinking. Leave blame, anger, resentment, guilt, and regret at the door, and simply look at "What is."

Every time an unpleasant emotion wanders through your mind, let it go and refocus on the facts of where you are, what your situation is, and what isn't working for you.

Then think of taking all of your "What is" information and dividing it into two "piles" - okay, lists! But I'm very visual so I'm seeing "piles of stuff" in my head!

One pile is the stuff you cannot change and over which you have no control. The other pile is all about what you ***can*** change and where you ***do*** have control - as much as we ever have, given that the Universe can throw those big boulders into the middle of our respective ponds whenever it takes the notion...

The point of the exercise is to get a solid grasp on your starting position. It is to help you see where you are right now, and then we'll begin to work on figuring out where you want to go.

Day 2 - "A journey of a thousand miles..."

It is said that, "A journey of a thousand miles begins with a single step." This is attributed to Lao-Tzu, a brilliant Chinese philosopher who wrote a lot about the Tao. More correctly, the proper translation from Chinese is "The journey of a thousand miles begins beneath one's feet."

At first glance, they might seem to have almost identical meanings. But in fact, each is quite different from the other.

First, let's take a look at the less-well-known but correct translation. "The journey of a thousand miles begins beneath one's feet." This beautiful statement is filled with optimism and hope. It's about looking at where you are right now, accepting what is, and leaving the past where it belongs.

It's about seeing what needs to change in your life. It's about preparing for forward movement and growth. It's empowering. It's filled with anticipation.

It leads straight to the more widely known version: "A journey of a thousand miles begins with a single step." This teaches patience, determination and perseverance. It teaches gentleness in the art of change.

It offers hope and encouragement to anyone who is on a difficult path, especially when there is the temptation to give up, or not even start in the first place.

Being aware of what's at that point in the distance will help you to decide where to place your foot with that first step. Each one thereafter takes you further away from where you are now, from what lies beneath your feet and moving you closer to where you want to be.

Do not fear putting your foot down in the wrong place. This happens sometimes when you look down at your feet, rather than ahead at your destination but you can correct the problem. Keep focused on the destination; your feet will follow your eyes.

Invitation: If you completed the suggested exercise yesterday, you might find something more to add to it by answering the questions below.

Take a good look at what lies beneath your feet. Where are you now? What do you need to accept about your situation? What is your current reality? What do you want to change about it?

It begins with that first step. Create a clear vision. Then keep putting one foot in front of the other and in time, you will be where you want to be.

Day 3 - If there's a way into a mess, there's a way out.

Oh, no! How did I get into this? How did this happen? My life was ticking along just fine - or maybe not all that fine, but it wasn't like *this*! It's a disaster!

Does this sound familiar? I'm sure we've all been there. Perhaps that's where you are right now. And if you are, the good news is that if you got into it, you can get out of it.

Okay, it's true there may be some aspects of your situation that you cannot change. If, for example, you're sitting in a car that you just wrapped around an enormous tree a moment ago, you can't rewind about ten seconds and take it all back. After all, life isn't like one big shoelace that you can just undo whenever you want. So you made some choices that have got you all tied up in knots and you don't know where to begin to fix it.

First of all, just for a moment, forget where you are. Forget the fact that you're seriously in the soup and look ahead. Never mind what's wrong just now; what do you want to be right? Come on, push aside all the bits that are upsetting, distressing, disturbing, or fill-in-the-blank. Yes, you *can*. *You* are in control of your thoughts. *You* get to choose what goes on in your head. Your life or the situation may *feel* out of control at the moment but it's temporary. The only constant is change, so hold onto that knowledge and begin by changing your thoughts.

Set all your worries to one side for a moment. Forget where you are, and see where you want to be. Just close your eyes and focus on what you want. Do *not* think about how you want this or that to stop, because then you're still focusing on what you *don't* want. Be very clear about this. Focus on what you *want*.

This is an extremely important difference and it is vital to your ending up where you want to be as quickly as possible. Firstly, it's because positive thoughts produce hundreds of times more energy than negative ones (so says science), which will make you feel better and get you moving again. Secondly, because the Law of Attraction is at work all the time, whether you're thinking about it or not. So if you focus on what you don't want, you'll only attract more of it.

You might have seen it in action if you experience anxiety. The more you dwell on being anxious, the more anxious you become. And before long, you're having full-blown panic attacks. Then you're terrified of another one so you stay in a constant state of heightened anxiety, thinking more and more anxious thoughts and presto - another panic attack.

So for example, don't be thinking, "I don't want to be anxious." Think, "I am calm." Don't think, "I wish I didn't have any debt." Think, "I am financially secure."

Once you've got the hang of it, it becomes quite simple to flip negative thoughts into positive ones. Then hold the vision. See what you want. Feel it, as if it's real. As you're looking to the future and seeing where you want to be, don't be thinking, "Thank heaven this situation is over!" - because then you're still focusing on "this situation"!

Every time you think of what's wrong, change that feeling, that thought, or that image into the vision of what you want and hold onto it for a few moments. Not only will it lift your spirits, it will also keep you focused, feeling positive and moving forward.

Invitation: As for more immediate solutions for "how to get out of this," find at least one thing you can do today to take a step toward the way out. Perhaps you've been so distracted by the problem(s), your house is a bit of a disaster or there's a ton of filing or unopened mail waiting for you.

Pick just one thing you think you can do today and do it. Make a dent in that mountain of laundry. Tidy up one room. Brush your hair. Do something. Anything. Just do one thing that begins to move you toward where you want to be. It doesn't have to be huge - but it can be, if you're up for it.

Perhaps your "something" is making a list of all the things you need or want to do and then each day, pick one and cross it off the list when you've done it. I've done that at very busy times in my life and I can't tell you how deliciously satisfying it is to be able to cross something off a list!

Commit to doing at least one of those 'somethings' every day. If you can do more than one, go for it. That's great! With each one that gets done, you'll feel better. Your confidence will grow, you'll begin to feel empowered, and you'll have more energy. And you know why? Because you'll be taking control of your life again.

The more you feel like you're in the driver's seat, the more you'll look through the windscreen and see that vision for your future. Every time you see it, it's not going to seem so far off in the distance. Every time you see it, that vision will become a little clearer. And that will only make it easier for you to know exactly which roads to take and where you need to turn in order to get there.

You might well be in a really enormous mess. But you can unwrap the car from that massive tree trunk. You can get the front end repaired or rebuilt. The tree will heal - and so will you.

Yeah, you got yourself into this. But you can put yourself back behind the wheel and get out of it, too - one mile at a time.

Just see where you want to be. Then hold that vision...

Day 4 - The Only Way Your Dreams Will Die Is If You Let Them

I know how it is when you don't have a dream. When you can't even begin to imagine something wonderful could happen to you. I know what it's like to think you've found your "dream come true," only to have it smashed into a zillion pieces right in front of your face.

And I know it can be scary to let yourself dream, because then you're leaving yourself open to disappointment. But if you never dream, how are you going to have a shot at being happy? How will you ever discover all the magnificence inside you that's just waiting for you to share it with the rest of us? How will you ever know all you could have had or been or done if you never take that chance?

Disappointment isn't much fun, it's true. But it's not the end of the world.

For now, I just want you to think about a dream. It can be really big, or just a little one. Whatever feels good for you will be just right. There's no excuse not to have one. And don't allow yourself to go to that victim place of "Poor me! I don't dare dream! Nothing good ever happens to me!" and more of that rubbish.

Being a victim does not serve you well. When you're in that place, you've chosen to give up your power, which leaves you *feeling* helpless, even though you really aren't. Don't go there. Together, we're on a mission to help you take back your power.

Start by creating a dream. It doesn't cost anything. And it doesn't even require any energy. It requires only a little imagination, a desire - perhaps just the little spark of one - and you can go to the most amazing places in your mind. And those places may become your reality. If you're gonna dream, dream Big. Why not? You have nothing to lose. And everything to gain.

Your dreams can motivate you to be better, to achieve more, to have, to be, to do what your heart desires. They feed the ambitions of your soul. They quench the thirst of your longing.

Without dreams, you will have nothing for which to strive, nothing to give you hope, nothing to which you can cling when the storms of life are tossing you from pillar to post.

It is true that some of your dreams will never come true. But you won't know which ones they are until you've made every effort, until you've done absolutely everything in your power to make them a reality. Giving up before then should not be an option.

The only way your dreams will die is if you let them.

Invitation: If you don't already have a dream or dreams in mind, this is your lucky day because you're about to have one - or as many as you want to create today! It's exciting to give birth to a dream! It becomes a focal point for your future. It brings hope and can light a fire under you and get you moving when you've been feeling stuck.

Perhaps resurrect one that you gave up a long time ago. What did you dream about when you were a kid? Even if it seems silly, don't disregard it. Perhaps there's a way to build it into your life in a way that works.

If you go blank when trying to come up with one, it might be helpful to look at what you've written about accepting what you can't change, and acknowledging what you can. What can you change about your life? What would you like to be different? Use that as a beginning point for building your dream.

Write about your dream in as much detail as you can. If you're not big on writing, you don't have to use whole sentences. Bullet points work. It's just important to get it all on paper. It helps to make it more real - more possible.

Then use magazines or go online and find images that represent your dream. The invitation is to create a mini vision board, just gather together pictures that remind you of what you want. Every time I re-do or add to my vision board, I put several photos on one page and then print it off so I can cut them up and stick them on the board.

You could just have a collection of photos on a printed page and put it where you can see it regularly, preferably several times a day.

Day 5 - From Goodbyes to Big Dreams

You're at a turning point. Ready to leave the past behind and make a fresh start. You've just come through a challenging time and you're wondering "What's next? And how do I get there?"

Perhaps you're experiencing an ending that you didn't want and it's time to begin again. Whatever that means...

Whatever lies behind you is a mixed blessing. There will have been good times and bad. Unfortunately, it's human nature to focus on the bad ones and minimise the good.

But thank heaven for the Spirit residing inside you. It's in there, quietly waiting for you to remember it, to focus on it, to remind you of the blessings in your life and to give you some perspective on your difficulties.

It's there, reminding you that it's ***always*** there, guiding you, gently nudging you in the direction of strength, peace, and compassion, and of spiritual growth and purity of love. It's there for you in your worst and most painful times, being the force that pulls you out of those terrible, dark holes. It's there for you in the best of times, saying, "Well done, you're on the right path!"

Your Spirit is always there, remembering you, assisting you. Perhaps today - and every day moving forward - you could be sure to remember your Spirit, too. Acknowledge its existence in you, its presence and influence in your life. It is who you are meant to be. It is your Highest Self.

Acknowledging your spirit is like speaking to yourself in the future, to the person you could become, or will become - if that's what you choose. You can be human and stumble here and there. That's not a problem. But your Spirit will keep holding out the hand that helps you up, and that keeps you moving forward.

Reflect on the past, whether it was mostly good or mostly not, and then do yourself a favour. Focus on the good bits. Remember a whole lot of them. Then dig for some more. Let go of the ones that hurt, or they'll just keep ripping at the wound and not allowing it to heal.

If it's a stretch to do that, tell yourself that you're at least ***willing*** to let it all go. This word opens the door a crack and begins to let in the Light of love and healing.

Thank your Spirit for its wisdom and guidance, which helped you through your challenges when you paid attention to it.

As for the times you neglected or ignored it, no doubt there were natural consequences for that so it will forgive you. Just take the lessons, and going forward, keep focusing on connecting with your Spirit. It will never steer you wrong.

Invitation: You may be quite happy to kiss the past goodbye. But before you do that, take a little time to allow it to leave you with the gifts you've forgotten it gave, and forgive it for having disappointed you along the way. Write about the gifts and about what you want to leave behind.

Think about this date one year from now. Write your answers to these questions: What would make it be a perfect day? What will you want to say about the previous year - from now until then? What will you have hoped to achieve, to be, to have changed about yourself and your life? Now is the time to visualise that perfect day, and what you want your circumstances to be at that time. Write about it in as much detail as you can, even if it's in bullet points.

Keep those notes handy because I'm inviting you to read them every morning before you dive into your day, preferably followed by at least a brief meditation during which you close your eyes and really feel that day, as if it is the day you're about to begin.

Most importantly, don't forget to Dream Big. Then, with a clear picture of that dream in your head, take your first steps into your future - your first steps toward making that dream come true!

Day 6 - Magnify The Magnificence!

Wow. Look at that. Another new day. Isn't it magnificent?

You might ask, "What's so magnificent? I have to do this and that and a bunch of other stuff I don't really want to do. Can I just go back to bed now please and call it a day?"

Or you might be focusing on recent or current challenges. Okay, so you have some difficult circumstances. You don't have to think about them all the time, and in fact, I would strongly advise against doing that. Your brain and body are far more closely linked that you might know.

"They" say we have 60,000-70,000 thoughts a day (I'd like to know who's counting. Do they use one of those little clicker counting things? You couldn't possibly click fast enough...!). Anyway, with every thought, your brain creates chemical messengers to ship out to every single one of your trillions of cells. All of your cells have little receptors on them, like lily pads that reach up and grab the memo as it sails past and there are your receptors, reading the memo, "Hm, what are we doing now? Okay, we're anxious! Right!" And then it tells the cell how to respond in anxiety.

The most recent statistics say that more than fifty percent of all deaths are caused by stress. And stress is not about what's going on outside of you; it's entirely about your internal response to the external factors. The more you think about your stress or your difficult circumstances or past emotional wounds or betrayals or trauma, the more you are dumping loads of negative energy and toxic biochemical responses into your body. Ultimately, this has the potential to cause significant illness.

The more you choose positive thoughts, the more positive energy you put into your body. So stop dwelling on your miseries and take some time every day to consider your magnificence, and the magnificence of this day.

What's so magnificent about today? Well, for one thing, you woke up. You're drawing breath. Think about the magnificence of that. Think about what your body is doing, all by itself, all the time, without any instruction from you.

Automatically, your heart keeps beating, flooding every part of your body with blood, with fresh oxygen to keep you alive. All of your organs, tissues, bones and muscles are functioning so you can do all kinds of things. You can move, create, communicate, work, play, enjoy time with special people, and live your life.

You're not thinking about it, but your body is very busy, doing millions of super cool things quietly behind the scenes, just like the camera crew, the director, producers, and that looooooong list of people you see in the credits but never see in the film. Without them, the film would not exist, no matter how much you pay the actors to show up.

Even if some parts of you are now absent or not working (or not as well as they used to do), you're still here and you're well enough that you're able to read this. Your brain, your eyes, your nervous system are all allowing you to absorb and understand what you're seeing. That's magnificent!

So this day is here, and it's also magnificent that *you* are here. Even if you aren't feeling it in this moment, it's still the truth. Just ask anyone who loves you or depends upon you, anyone who looks forward to seeing you, hearing from you. They'll tell you that it's magnificent you're here.

And that's because *you're* magnificent! There's no one else just like you. Yeah, I know, you've heard that before. We've all heard that before. But do you ever really think about it? You're not replaceable. You're the only "you" who will ever exist. No one else will ever create anything the way you do, whether it's a conversation, a piece of art, the way you cook, the life you live, the family you build, or the way you contribute to friendships, to the world, or to your own little corner of it. You matter to many people. You mean the world to some. Because you're magnificent.

Invitation: Today isn't just another day. Today is a magnificent, precious gift from the universe. You've never seen *this* day before. Don't just sit there staring at it, admiring the pretty big bow, the lovely ribbon and beautiful wrapping paper, and wondering what's inside. Go on, open it up and see!

It's already a magnificent day, just because it's arrived and just because you're here. Imagine what it could be if you magnify the magnificence by letting your Spirit tear into that gift! Give it a try!

Write about what makes today magnificent, or what you could do to appreciate its magnificence.

Write about what makes you magnificent, too. You might be at the bottom of a big dark hole but you know what? That's the best time to rummage around inside yourself and find the brightest and best parts of you that you've forgotten existed.

Find your magnificence and write about it. Then go off and magnify the magnificence of the day by showing up as magnificently as you can.

And this evening, write about how much better your day was for having seen it - and you - as magnificent!

Day 7 - Positively positive

I don't read the paper. I don't listen to the news. In fact, I'll go a step further. I **won't** read the paper and I **won't** listen to the news. There's so much torment and tragedy, murder and misery, nothing but story after story about man's inhumanity to man, about horrible accidents, Acts of God that cause death and destruction. Do I really need to hear every possible rotten, awful thing that has happened out there? Does it add anything to my life? Will I be worse off for not knowing about these terrible incidents?

No.

I figure that if there's anything I really need to know, like the sky is falling or Armageddon's happening after dinner on Tuesday, someone will tell me.

I told a journalist friend once that I ought to start up a newspaper that was full of only good news. He said it wouldn't sell because people want the blood and guts (my words, not his, but that was the general idea). He said good news doesn't (or wouldn't) sell papers.

I think it would. Some of us want to be surrounded by positivity. Some of us want to know the good news, the happy events, the wonderful moments and miracles that are happening in the world. Some of us want to be uplifted by the beauty that exists in the perfect stories of love and kindness that are taking place around us, especially when they happen between strangers.

Some of us prefer to be connected with light and lovely positive energy that allows growth and movement, rather than heavy, oppressive negative energy that keeps us stuck and stagnant. I refuse to give attention to the negatives in my life or my environment, above and beyond what is absolutely essential in order to deal with certain issues.

Beyond that, negative thoughts are chased away and replaced by positive ones. If I find myself thinking about anything that is distressing or upsetting - particularly if it's nothing I am able to change - I dismiss it, focusing instead on what I want - and *not* on what I don't want.

I insist on positivity in my relationships and in how I spend my time - in everything I do. I avoid negativity, negative people, situations, anything toxic. There is no room for any of that in my life.

Do you have people coming to you and dumping their miseries on your lap on a regular basis? I mean the ones who walk away saying, "Oh I feel so much better" and you feel like something you'd scrape off your shoe...And they do it over and over again, never really changing anything about their lives, they just want to complain.

There are probably going to be some family or other relationships over which you think you have no control, and you feel like you must stay stuck in them. I'm here to tell you that you do not.

Even if you don't officially end a relationship, you can change the dynamics by speaking your truth, saying how you feel, by drawing clear boundaries around taboo subjects or not tolerating being treated in certain ways. You can expect some "push back" but the more you stand up for yourself and refuse to tolerate disrespect, toxic behaviour, the better you will feel about yourself.

Remember: You are a powerful being, and you do not have to allow any more destruction of your time or energy in this life.

Why would you choose to do any other way to live? Unless, of course, you have some burning desire to destroy your life, your happiness and wellbeing.

You have complete control over what you think and how you respond to anyone or anything. You have complete control in deciding where to focus your attention and energy. You can choose to make your life better - or worse.

I know what I'm choosing. How about you?

Invitation: Take stock of areas of your lifestyle or relationships where there is negativity. Write a list of all of it. Don't forget things like the kinds of television shows you watch or other influences to which you are subjected - e.g. do you watch a lot of real life stories of murder? Do you eat a lot of junk food? Do you smoke? Live in a stressful environment? What about exercise?

Once you've got a list of as many areas of negativity as possible, consider where you can make changes. Don't load yourself up with so many that you feel overwhelmed. But at least once you're aware of them, you can begin to change your habits and clean things up in your field of energy (i.e. all aspects of your life) so that you're decreasing the negativity around you and increasing the positivity.

Here's a delicious little visualisation exercise or meditation that I recommend you do at least once a day. Imagine yourself immersed in sparkling, radiant, shimmering, positive energy of the purest kind. You are bathed in it. Delight in how wonderful it feels.

Then think about the negative aspects of your life. Notice the difference in how it feels. It's not very pleasant. Find a way that works for you to see those aspects disappearing. Perhaps you'll envision packing them up in an airtight locked container and chucking it into the ocean or sending it out into the universe. Maybe you'll just surround those aspects of your life with love and light and the best intentions for healing.

Whatever works for you, find a way to release the negativity and keep it outside of your happy, sparkling energy and just enjoy sitting in that lovely peaceful place for as long as you like.

This is also a terrific option for times when you're feeling particularly stressed, anxious, or depressed. Just close your eyes, and while taking a few slow, deep breaths, focus on being immersed in sparkling, radiant, positive energy. See it keeping negativity away from you and just allow yourself to reconnect with a sense of peace.

Day 8 - A Little Faith and A Lot of Patience...

Things might be awful for you right now. I hope not, but of course Life does have a way of being miserable sometimes. And in some cases, it can go on a very long time.

It's not as miserable when you have some control over the situation, when you can actively do something to make it better, to change it in some way and get back to a happier place. But it really sucks when it's pretty much out of your hands.

In those cases, all you can really do is change yourself, your own attitudes and responses to what's happening.

Trust me, I do understand complete and utter despair. I know what it is to suffer, so I really do understand just how tough things can be sometimes.

When it gets like that for you, you've got to hang onto faith. Be patient and trust that in time, things will get better. Even if you've got to dig deep to find faith and patience, do it. Don't give up.

Although it doesn't always feel like it, you have control over what goes on in your head. You can choose to think about how awful your situation is, and how dark and miserable things are right now, and how they're just going to stay that way.

Or you can look ahead and have faith that things will change, that the Wheel of Life will soon begin to turn in your favour again. You can trust that there will be a bit of good news tomorrow or next week, that you'll see the first signs of improvement in your situation. Because it *will* come, you know. Nothing stays the same forever. And if you're like I used to be, you'll say, "Yeah, I know. It can get worse!"

And yes, that's a possibility. But equally, it also means that things can get better. If you're going to give some time and energy to the negative, the positive deserves at least the same attention. Be fair and give it equal time. In fact, give it a *lot* more time.

Then find a little patience. If you've lost that too, then make some more. You do it by remembering other times when things were dark and horrible, but then they got better. Come on, don't tell me that every single minute of your whole existence since birth has been awful. Even if there has been a lot of misery, if there have been many hardships, some of them will have made room for brighter days in the past.

And I'll bet that when you were in the soup back then, you might not have thought it would ever get better. But it did. And it'll get better again. You create faith and you create patience by choosing to welcome them into your thoughts, by opening your mind, your heart, your life to them and telling yourself - no, by *insisting* - that your situation will improve.

The Universe doesn't always give us what we want. But it always gives us what we need. And if you need courage, strength, faith or patience, even if you have to look for them, you will always find them because they are always there inside you, just waiting for you discover them.

Invitation: Write or list times in your life when you didn't believe that things could get better, but they did. Write about times when you didn't think you could get through something but you did. Write or list what you did that helped and look at the roles that faith and patience played in those situations - or if they were lacking, how they might have made a difference.

Remember the choices you made that led to you getting through it, or feeling better, or improving the situation in some way.

Then write or list ways in which your current situation could turn around and be better. Look for reasons to have faith and be patient. Look for possibilities. Think outside the box.

Day 9 - Hope Is A State of Mind

I'll bet you know what it is to be hopeful. And I'll bet you know what it is to feel completely hopeless, too. It's pretty miserable, to say the least. I've always said you can live a long time on just a little bit of hope. And when it's gone, it can feel like life isn't worth living.

But do you want to hear one of the coolest things about hope? It's a choice. It's a decision. If you want it, you can have all you want. When there's an incident that seems to wipe out the last of it, you can refill any time you like. It's up to you to decide whether or not to give up, to throw in the towel and say that's it, that's all, you're baked, you're done.

You're always free to do that, but it's a miserable place to live. The world is a much brighter place when you can hope that things will improve. And you know what? They always do.

Sure, sometimes they get a whole lot worse before they get better. I'm way too familiar with ***that*** story. But eventually, they *will* improve. That's because things are always changing. It's the only constant. In that, you can trust.

Okay, so at least there is that little tidbit to get you through when things aren't going your way and you want to check out, give up, go home, chuck your toys out the cot and cry. You can always tell yourself you just have to be patient, wait your turn, or wait till the sun comes up on your life again, because it will, whatever else is going on, no matter how dark and dismal it is.

Yeah, I can just hear you telling me how hard it is to feel hopeful when you're life has just thrown up all over itself. Especially if it's been doing it for quite a while. Maybe even years. And I know *that* story all too well, too.

But so what if it's hard to be hopeful? Do it anyway. Dig a little deeper. It's in there somewhere. It's just buried under some other stuff but poke around, you'll find the hope you need because it's in the thoughts that you choose to think.

You might be thinking I don't know just how bad it is for you right now, or how bad it might have been, or could get. I'm not you, but I've had more than my share of troubles and I can assure you, I do understand the generalities, if not the specifics.

I could tell you about loads of times I wanted to give up. I know fear. I know threat. I know suffering. I know despair and desperation.

I know what it is to have a life-threatening illness and get so fed up with it I had a plan to check out because I couldn't take the suffering any more.

And I didn't want my family to have to watch it any longer either. I figured they'd all be better off without me. I was pretty sure my children had all had enough of wondering which day they'd come home from school and find me dead.

I had a plan and I wasn't telling anyone. I knew from my social work training that this meant I was pretty "high risk" in terms of carrying out my plan for suicide but I didn't care. I wasn't just toying with the idea. I was "dead serious." I'd found a way out and all I felt when I thought about it was sweet relief. I was just waiting for the right time.

In the meantime, my patients needed me. As a homeopath, I was making them well. I was healing and helping, making a difference in their lives, still contributing, and my own suffering made it that much more important for me to carry on and remove theirs as long as I could stand to keep breathing.

They never knew it, but they were the reason why I chose to have hope that I would be well again someday, that I would at least find my way to a place where I could function again, even if not in perfect health.

After a few weeks of chewing on when I was going to carry out my foolproof plan to end my miserable existence, my digging for hope paid off. Finally, I saw the faintest little light at the end of the tunnel. I decided that I mustn't give up. Maybe I wouldn't just keep suffering until I was blissfully taken to an early grave. Maybe there would be a cure or some improvement.

And maybe not. But it was my choice, my prerogative to hope that I might get better someday. I made the decision to fight.

And so I fought. I fought for several more years until finally, there was an answer. There was healing and I've had many more happy and healthy years on the planet - all because I chose hope.

Invitation: Write about whatever came up for you on reading this passage. What kinds of thoughts and feelings did you have? How did it impact you? Did it change how you view hope? Did it reinforce thoughts you had already? Has it allowed you to shift to a more hopeful place?.

Day 10 -There is No Strength Store. You've Already Got All You Need.

There's a big difference between intelligence and ability, and knowledge and experience. Intelligence and ability speak about your potential; knowledge and experience speak about how far you've come in reaching it.

You wouldn't take a kid from kindergarten and stick him in university. That little kid needs to discover a lot about himself. He needs to learn a lot of information in between. As he progresses through his life, he is confronted with problems and countless places where he does not know what to do next. He builds on what he knows from his learning and experience, whether in school, at home or anywhere else.

If you've found yourself in the bottom of a pit where you feel helpless or powerless, if you're having a meltdown, a depression, if you're falling apart or just having some trouble coping and all of this makes you *believe* you're not strong, it doesn't mean you really aren't.

Perhaps your life has been ticking along just great for most of it and you've been lucky enough not to have had to cope with a lot of grief and misery before now, so you think you're not strong - but really, you just haven't had to be until now.

Or perhaps you've been slammed by too many problems at once; you were broadsided and it's taking a while to recover and you can't figure out why you always coped before but you're not coping very well right now. It's okay to be overwhelmed for now but it doesn't mean you're not strong.

Since I was a young adult, people have told me how "strong" I am. And sometimes people tell me they aren't as strong as I am - and even worse, they say they "never could be."

Well, first of all, I suppose if that's what they believe, that's what they'll get. And they'll never discover certain truths about strength, or their own capabilities

I can tell you that back in those early days as an adult, struggling as a single parent with a mess of other insanity in my life, I didn't feel strong at all. I was alone. I didn't have a support system and I had to figure it out for myself. I fought my way through some pretty awful situations and still held things together on the outside. But I was a complete mess on the inside.

I was 19, divorced, with a ten-month-old baby to raise by myself as her father had been transferred to another province. Those were actually the least of my challenges - but they were what made me begin to overcome the rest of the nightmare I was living.

To be honest, things got a whole lot worse for a long time before they ever got better - I had more kids, more toxic relationships, ill health - but all the while I was discovering the first and most important truth about strength. I learned that until you need it, it's one of those untapped resources inside yourself. It's not like you don't have any and you have to go to the Strength Store to get some so that presto, you're strong. It's something you find inside yourself - if you want it or if you need it badly enough.

The most important truth about strength is this: ***It is a decision, really. Simple as that.*** You create it when you make the decision to that you will never give up on yourself and your ability to get where you want to be. And that means there is a never-ending supply of strength available to you.

At times, you may be worn out, overwhelmed, and needing a 'time out' to refill that supply. That's okay. Be gentle with yourself and trust that you'll connect with your strength once again after you have a little rest, or when you borrow a little from others, much like boosting a car battery.

It's often easier to be strong when there is someone else relying on you, someone for whom you feel responsible - even pets fill this role. Studies prove that people who have pets to look after will recover from illness or injury a lot quicker than people who have no one relying on them.

But to dig deep and find your strength because *you* need it is one of the greatest gifts you can give yourself.

Another important truth about strength is that like everything else in life, it must be balanced. It's great to find your strength. But not at the expense of your vulnerability. It is okay to need, to lean, to accept help when it is offered, and to ask for it, too. None of that should be seen as weakness. It takes strength to allow others to see your vulnerability.

So the next time you catch yourself saying you're not strong, or you're not as strong as someone else, just remember the potential is there. The Strength Store isn't out here somewhere; it's right there inside you. It may take a little practice to find it, but you've already got all the strength you'll ever need.

<u>Invitation:</u> Write or list times or events in your life when you didn't think you had the strength to deal with a particular situation. You didn't think you had the tools or whatever it took to get through it. But you did. What did you do? What were the strategies you used? Where did you turn for support (remember: asking for support is a sign of strength, not a sign of weakness!)?

Look at all the ways in which you found strength that you didn't think you had. Then write about some of the ways in which you can begin to turn things around now. One of the most important ways to begin to find your strength is that every time you hear yourself say or think, "I can't!" you must stop yourself and say, "Yes! I can! And I will!"

And if you don't know how to do it - whatever "it" is - tell yourself, "I will figure it out! I will find the answers!" Those kinds of empowering thoughts can go a long way toward pulling you out of a victim, helpless, weak place of "I can't." And before you know it, you ***will***!

Day 11 - You Always Have A Choice

I know how it is to feel trapped. I know how it is to feel helpless. Powerless. Like there's no way out, and nowhere to go even if you *could* get "out" (wherever that is or whatever that means). It's so easy to go with the negative thoughts and believe that you're stuck.

But it is only a belief. And the beauty of that - and the *power* in that - is that you can change your beliefs. And with that, you can change your feelings, too.

If, for example, you're trapped in an unhappy home environment, you can still choose to focus on the blessings in your life. You can still choose to meditate and take yourself to a peaceful, restful place in your mind (which can do a lot to help reduce the stress you feel in general). You can still choose to begin finding solutions to the problems, or looking for a way to change that environment or to leave it altogether.

It's so easy to feel like you have no control over your life. Sometimes we feel like helpless victims who have ended up in a terrible position because of someone else's decisions, needs, feelings, expectations, etc. It's so easy to blame others and not recognise the part we played in things turning out as they have. In doing this, however, we give away our power. In putting the blame elsewhere, we say "I don't have the ability to choose for myself or make my own decisions or say 'no' or insist on doing something the way I want it done." We say, "Here, you can have control over my life. Take my power. Please."

But that's probably because you weren't aware that it's okay to keep your power and make your choices and stop worrying about trying to live up to what everyone else needs, wants, or expects you to do. You've always got one of the most powerful tools in the world. You have the ability to make choices. Your own choices have led you to where you are right now. Yes, you had a hand in it, whether it's a good place or not, or a little of both. You made choices that landed you exactly where you stand in your life at this moment.

And if you're not happy with it, think about how that knowledge can give you back the power you didn't think you had! You have the power to make a different set of choices, and end up on a path that is of *your* choosing.

Sure, the Universe will lob stuff at you and throw obstacles in your path. That's its job. Yours is to overcome them, to make choices that will navigate your way around them, over them, through them, and find your authentic self - and the peace and happiness that will come from that journey.

It all begins with every choice you make. Big ones, little ones - all of them pack a whole lot of your own personal power so take careful aim before releasing them to the Universe. Remember that old saying, "Be careful what you wish for"...

Invitation: Look at your current situation or an aspect of your life that you find to be challenging. Look at the long list of circumstances that had to unfold in order for that situation to occur.

Pick apart those circumstances and look at the decisions that went into them. Be brutally honest with yourself about the role you played. You didn't get here because of someone else. You got here because of you. Even if you didn't make any decisions and left everything up to someone else so you could now point the finger and say, "See the mess you made for us?" that still doesn't wash, because you made the decision to leave it to someone else. If you gave up your voice, that was your choice.

The more you can take ownership of how you ended up in situations you don't like, the more you take control of your life and will be able to create something better.

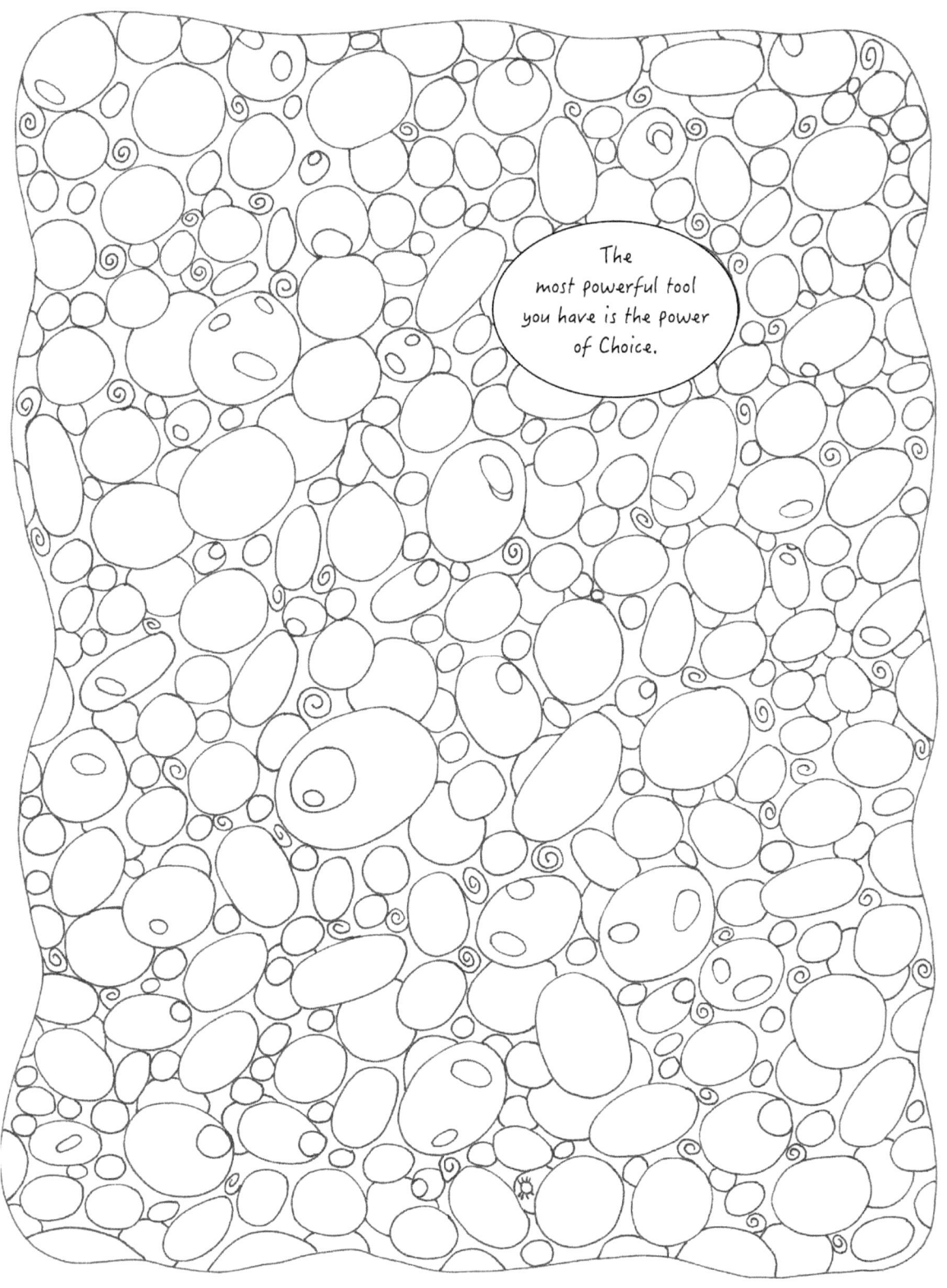

Day 12 - Make It Be A Beautiful New Day...

The sun is rising, casting a soft, rosy glow across the cool grey sky, gently warming all it surveys as it quietly welcomes us to yet another new day.

Sleepily, we climb out of our comfortable cocoons, yawning and stretching as we shuffle off to the kitchen for that hot cup of tea or that steaming mug of coffee, sliding ourselves into our lives for one more morning, not noticing the glorious New Day that lies before us, brimming over with possibilities and joy just waiting to be discovered.

Instead, thoughts and images of what needs to be done stumble through the fog of semi-consciousness as the day begins to unfold. *Gotta get to work...The children need feeding and dressing...I hope their homework was really all done...The toilets need cleaning...There's no food in the fridge...The house is a mess...Oh, the laundry...I need to make that appointment...There are all those repairs that need doing...*

And on and on it goes...your endless list of Stuff To Do. Before you're even functional or have had a bit of breakfast, you're already weighted down by responsibility and have to, ought to, should and must.

And then there's the added Really Difficult Stuff. The relationship that needs life support and is in the Intensive Care Unit. The blazing row you had last night, and didn't resolve. The teenager who's rebelling. Or the one who has been missing for months. The job you lost. And your house might be next. The bad news you're anticipating at the doctor's office. The funeral you have to attend on Thursday. The chemotherapy you're facing. Your widowed parent who is fragile and ailing. You get the idea.

So how can days like that be filled with possibilities and joy just waiting to be discovered? How on earth are you supposed to notice that soft, rosy glow outside, that wonderful sense of newness and excitement that it holds as it spreads its smiling warmth across everything in its path?

You just do. It doesn't discount any of the Stuff that demands your attention, or insists upon cramming itself down your throat. It doesn't mean the painful parts of your life will vanish. It just means that you must not forget the blessings because they're as real a part of your life as the parts that hurt or feel like an enormous burden, and which will consume you, if you let them.

One of those blessings is the ability to choose what occupies your thoughts, and at least some of your time. It is the ability to give yourself permission to have a little fun, to do something that makes you happy, that makes you feel good, or that lets you take some time to reconnect with yourself.

When you inject some lightness and positivity into your life, you feel more able to cope with the challenges. You can close your eyes for a few moments at any time in the midst of the most miserable day and think about someone or something wonderful. And if you stay focused on that image and those feelings, even for just a few moments, you're bound to find a little respite from your worries.

No matter how dark and miserable your life might be, there are blessings, too, and opportunities to make it a better day. Just pause for a few moments and notice that rosy, glowing sunrise as it gently reminds you that there is another New Day, another chance for you to reconnect with yourself and with all the blessings the world has to offer. Allow its warmth to fill your soul, awakening beautiful old memories that will nourish you, urging you to create equally beautiful new ones, now. Today. And every day.

Invitation: Start a list of things you can do that you would enjoy and that would make you feel better and do something from that list every day. Read a favourite novel - again. Dust off the deck of cards for a game of rummy with your partner. Soak your feet. Look through old photographs. Work on a scrapbook.

It doesn't take much time in a day to give yourself a break from your stresses, even if it's only as long as it takes to spend a few moments here and there, thinking about what's important to you, about the people who matter to you.

Day 13 - Changing What You Believe Will Change How You React

In the 1950s, a psychologist called Albert Ellis developed Rational Emotive Therapy. It was the basis for what we now call cognitive behavioural therapy, which is commonly used in the treatment of depression, anxiety and various other disorders.It deals with how our thoughts affect our emotions. If we change our thoughts, we can change our emotional responses.

Ellis came up with the ABC Theory - A is the action or event, which leads to B, your belief about the action, which leads to C - the consequent emotion about the event. Ellis said that we think we skip from A to C. For example, this particular thing happens, and this is how I feel about it - which then dictates your response to the situation.

But that is not how it works. The event does not cause the emotion; it is what you believe about the event or a situation that will directly, and immediately affect how you feel, and you feelings will be the foundation of your behaviour.

Hidden somewhere in between the event and the emotion, there is a belief about the event, and this is what leads to the emotion. If we can identify what that belief is, we have the power to change the emotion that follows. As simple as this seems to be, this is one of the most empowering bits of knowledge you can ever possess.

As an example of just how powerful this theory can be, let's take a look at how two very different people might respond to being hit by a partner.

Let's say a woman grew up in a home where there was a lot of physical abuse and she witnessed her parents hitting each other on a regular basis. Eventually, she marries and one day her husband slaps her across the face. She might be angry but she isn't likely to do a whole lot about it.

Let's say a woman grew up in a home where everyone was always respectful and loving. One day, her husband hits her. She is likely to be shocked, angry, indignant, hurt, and might well ring police or pack a bag and leave.

On the surface, it might look to each of these women that the slap leads to the reaction. But it's not. It's what each of them believes about the slap that leads to the reaction. The first woman believes this is normal behaviour. She doesn't have to like it but to her, it's what married people do so she's not likely to do anything about it.

But to the second one, this is a completely shock. She believes this is absolutely not normal. She believes love and marriage have nothing to do with being slapped. So she isn't about to tolerate it. Jammed in between the slap and the way each woman responds is a belief about it. The belief happens in a nanosecond and is what drives the behaviour that follows.

Our beliefs shape our thoughts. Our thoughts shape our choices. And our choices shape our lives. If we can change our beliefs about ourselves, and our situations, then we change our choices, and ultimately, we change our lives.

Invitation: When you're struggling with unpleasant emotions, perhaps it will help you to back up and look at the initial event or situation that led to those feelings. Examine your beliefs about the situation. If you can change what you believe, and put a more positive spin on it, you may well find that you begin to feel better.

Go on. Give it a try. It won't happen overnight but if you keep reinforcing those new beliefs, eventually they'll stick!

Your beliefs shape your thoughts. Your thoughts shape your choices. Your choices shape your life. If you want to change your life, you must begin by changing what you believe.

Day 14 - Focus on What You Want, Not on What You Don't Want

I would imagine that the things you don't want are things that would make you feel miserable or unhappy in some way. You don't want to lose your job because there'd be all those obvious fears and worries. You don't want to lose your relationship because you'd be unhappy. Or you're thinking about how you hate being on your own and wish you had a 'special someone'. Or, or, or... the point is, there are reasons why you don't want 'it', whatever 'it' is.

The Law of Attraction says that like attracts like. What you think about, you bring about. Positive or negative, whether you want it or not, if you keep thinking about it, you will attract it to yourself.

But if you don't want to believe that there is such a law in existence, look at it this way: If all you think about is what you don't want, it'll be harder for you to see opportunities for you to get what you ***do*** want. It's that simple.

Imagine this: You're really upset about something. You're having a dreadful day or a dreadful bunch of days. Maybe your relationship is in the toilet, or your job is threatened by cutbacks or your health is bad - or perhaps you're stuck with all three. You've got all these worries on your mind. And you're not very hungry and don't really care about food or meal planning but your fridge is empty and it's getting a little skinny in the cupboards, too.

So you drag yourself off to the supermarket, get a trolley and aimlessly wander up and down the aisles. You're thinking about the relationship problems, the arguments, the hurt feelings, the question of whether or not to separate and what that might entail.

You're wondering if you could get another job but probably not in the current economy and then what would you do.... you're feeling tired and your back hurts and your head aches and you're having a lot of indigestion lately.

And there are you, not giving a rat's @$$ about the shopping and you're wandering up and down the aisles, not caring what you buy, staring at numerous tins, packets and boxes on the shelves but not really seeing them. Occasionally grabbing something familiar and chucking it in the trolley but your mind is only focused on what you don't want, what you're worried about.

You are not seeing all the opportunities for great meals that are right there in front of you. You're not thinking of the simplest ones, let alone the ones that take a little more time and effort but are so worth of every bit of it. You're not seeing the possibilities that are fairly leaping off the shelves at you, because you're so distracted and preoccupied with your worries, you can't see anything else around you. So you'll grab a box of biscuits or a tin of soup, boring and uninspiring things that reflect your state of mind as well as your complete and utter lack of interest in food or cooking. They reflect how you feel about your life.

And to make matters worse, not only do you bypass a million fantastic opportunities during your time in the supermarket, once you're home, you discover that you still don't really have much to eat besides the minimal selection of boring and uninspiring things you chucked into the trolley because you couldn't be bothered to open your eyes, look around and give your attention to the thousands of products that were right there in front of you.

It is the same with Life. If you're only focusing on the things you do not want, and that do not make you happy, you will have no appetite or enthusiasm for the possibilities that are all around you and in fact, you won't even see them. If you wish you had a better job or an opportunity of some kind, but you don't believe you could find one, you are not likely to see one, even if lands right in front of your feet. It's like going through life wearing blinders. You will only see what you want to see, and if you don't believe you will see anything good, then you won't see it, full stop.

It is essential to keep your eye on where you want to be and the more you do this, the more you will find the determination to keep focusing on it. When you do this, your intentions become sharper, stronger, and you will begin to see the opportunities that will help you get to where you want to be.

You want vegetables. Okay. Think about vegetables. Which vegetables do you want? How do you want them prepared? Stir-fried? In a soup? In a stew? A salad?

Focus on those vegetables. And as you do this, you will begin to see the possibilities, an idea or two, a recipe you haven't made in ages. The ideas will begin to come to you. Keep shoving away your worries, because worrying is just a prayer for the negative. It wastes your time and energy; it accomplishes nothing, other than to derail you and keep you stuck. You won't even be thinking about vegetables at all, much less thinking of ways to prepare them and what else you need for that recipe.

Instead, you'll be staring at a months-old tin of tasteless chicken soup with noodles so soggy they'll fall apart when you look at them sideways.

Life will keep throwing stuff at you that you don't want. It's your job not to let it knock you off balance. It's your job to steel yourself against it by focusing on those vegetables and the countless opportunities that are right there, just waiting to be noticed.

If you keep thinking your life is boring and uninspiring, that's exactly what it will be. It's your job to make it be interesting and inspiring. It's also your right and your privilege - and it is well within your power, whatever your circumstances, because the one constant about life is 'change'. It is inevitable. But how your life changes is entirely up to ***you***.

Focus on what you want, and ***not*** on what you ***don't*** want. Refuse to be derailed. Refuse to give the negatives your attention. Insist that you will have, be, or do whatever it is your heart desires. In doing so, your eyes will automatically be open to spotting whatever opportunities are available to help you achieve your goals, just as they will automatically be closed to them when you are not remotely receptive.

You've got the power and ability to change your thoughts and refocus - because *you* control every single one of them. And if you allow them to knock you off course, simply refocus again. With practice, it gets very easy to do.

Keep your eye on the prize. Then watch for the opportunities that will help you win it.

Invitation: Make a list of what you want. Be as specific as possible. What would make you happy? What would light up your life? Are there goals you'd like to achieve?

Then one at a time, look at each item. Write the thoughts that come to mind when you think about it. Are there negatives? Doubts? Self-defeating thoughts? "I can't," or "I'll never be able to..." or "How will I..."

Wherever you've found negative thoughts, make a new list that turns them into something positive. For example, "I don't know how to..." - you can change this to "I'll learn how to..."

And as for "I can't," that's one of the worst sentences in the world! Do not allow yourself to use it ever again - especially for something you've not yet even attempted to do! Go through your list and write lots of positive thoughts about each item, or at least thoughts that are progressive, like, "I'm willing to learn..." Take that list of negatives and destroy it. Burn it. Shred it. And do this mentally every time you catch yourself with one of those self-destructive notions wandering through your head.

Day 15 - No One Can Ever "Make You Feel" Anything.

"He makes me so angry!" "You make me jealous when you see your friends!" "I'll make her feel so guilty for this..." "Oh, I'm so sorry I hurt your feelings!"

These are the kinds of statements many people make on a regular basis. And that's because they believe it's possible for one person to have control over the feelings of another.

Well, I'm here to tell you it is absolutely ***not*** possible.

"But wait!" you might say, able to give me a long list of examples about this person or that one who knows how to push your buttons, knows exactly which triggers will get what reactions from you. They know how to wind you up and my goodness, do they ever go for it when they really want to upset you! So can I possibly say that no one else has any control over your feelings?

I can say it because it's the truth. Those people have learned that if they say or do something in particular, you will react in a certain way. You have taught them that if they do "this," then you will do "that." It's that simple. Those people do not "make" you react the way you do. Your reactions are your own choice. Every single time.

You may be familiar with the work of Ivan Pavlov. In the late 1800s, while doing research on aspects of the digestion of dogs, he ended up becoming famous for the "conditioned reflex". He noticed that dogs salivate just before they are given their food. Pavlov began ringing a bell and then feeding the dogs. Soon the dogs were salivating as soon as they heard the bell - even when there was no food present.

A ringing bell would not normally have induced such a response because it had nothing to do with food. The bell, in and of itself, had no power to make the dogs salivate. It's just that the dogs had learned to associate that sound with being fed.

And so it is with every single occasion upon which you hear yourself saying that someone makes you feel this or that. Those people have simply learned what your response will be when they say or do something in particular. Whatever might be at the root of your unhappy feelings and reactions is up to you to discover and heal.

If you believe that other people "make you feel" angry, guilty etc., you're handing them your power on a silver platter. You're saying, "I'm not in control of my life or my feelings."

But you can take back that control the moment you accept that your feelings are entirely in your hands. You get to decide how you will react. If people are used to you being angry in a certain situation, and that is their desired response, you can always choose to keep your temper and even if you do feel angry, you can choose to keep it to yourself and let them see only a calm exterior.

This really throws people who are used "pushing your buttons" and "making" you react in a way. But when you change your reaction, suddenly, their old tactics aren't working. Commonly, their response is to try harder to make you be the way you used to be. So they might step up their efforts to get you to react in the old way. They might push harder, throw more barbs, waiting to see how long it takes for you to react the way you used to do.

If you continue to remain calm (at least outwardly), eventually they'll give up because they're no longer getting the desired response. That's because they have no control over your feelings at all. They never did. The simple truth is that they had only learned that they could expect certain behaviours from you in a particular set of circumstances. They just never realised that you were always free to change what those behaviours would be.

But you can teach them something else now. You can begin by reacting in ways that do not give them the desired response. Soon they will learn that they cannot "push your buttons." They'll learn that they do ***not*** have any control over your feelings, and you'll learn that, too. It's one of the most empowering bits of information you will ever have.

Invitation: List some people or situations in your life about which you would normally say, "He/She/It makes me feel _____." It is helpful to be as detailed as you can with this exercise. Put yourself in those situations. Write how you feel, what your thoughts are, or anything that will help you to fully connect with how you feel when they happen.

Then go through the list, one item at a time, thoroughly considering how you would rather react. Write about your preferred responses, and notice how you feel as you think about them. Can you feel yourself becoming calmer, or feeling stronger, more in control of yourself and your life, and more empowered?

Spend some time visualising those situations with your new responses. Play them out in your mind as best you can, and begin to see yourself acting on them.

Remember, Rome wasn't built in a day. If you slip back into old habits, be gentle with yourself. Just notice where you slid, and as soon as you catch yourself going back to those old, unhealthy reactions, just stop. Walk away or politely but firmly end the conversation, do whatever you need to do so the situation doesn't go any further.

Collect your thoughts, remember the response you prefer, and try again next time. The more you do this, the easier it gets, as you develop confidence.

Be prepared; some people won't like the "new you" and they will likely try harder to get you to respond the way you used to do. They don't know what to do with your new behaviour; they can feel that they don't have the control over you that both of you thought they had.

As they step up their efforts to make you be the way you used to be, it might feel like you're being poked with a sharp stick! But stay the course; remember that you are in control of how you choose to react.

No one can make you feel anything. No one can push your buttons. You are always in control of your feelings.

Day 16 - On Becoming Empowered

Let's talk about empowerment.

Consider the example of a husband who "won't let" his wife see certain people, wear certain clothing or go somewhere that doesn't meet with his approval. It is important to remember - always - that other people have only as much control over you as you give them. Therefore, this husband says, "You're not allowed to see Suzy."

Perhaps Suzy is single, beautiful and has lots of men around and the husband is afraid his wife will leave him for one of them. Or perhaps Suzy doesn't like him and she's not afraid to show it, so he's afraid she'll convince his wife to leave him. All of his controlling behaviour (which is emotional abuse) is about a fear of being abandoned. If he can keep his wife on a short leash, and under his control, he will never be left alone.

Whatever his reasons, he attempts to control his wife by saying she's "not allowed" to see Suzy. The ball is now in his wife's court. She's actually got more power than she realises. **She** is now the one with all the control. She's the one who decides if she'll go along with what he wants (thereby giving the control back to him), or if she will keep the control and do what she believes is right for her.

If she chooses to keep her power and see the forbidden friend, Suzy, she could remind her husband that she is a grown woman and is entitled to make her own decisions about the people she chooses to see. She could remind him that she does not make his decisions for him, nor does pick his friends for him.

Whether it's about friends or clothes or make-up or anything else, the bottom line is the same. She could tell him that the more he tells her what to do, or not to do, the more it will push her away because he is being disrespectful of her.

I'm not suggesting that such a response is going to make him happy, or that he'll suddenly back down. He might, but if she's given him the control all along, and then suddenly she changes the "rules", it's more likely that he'll step up his efforts to make her be the way she used to be. He'll probably become more forceful and use intimidation tactics to get her to comply with his wishes.

In that instance, she has to be like a parent to a stubborn child and just be firm and consistent. If she isn't, as soon as she caves, he learns that he just has to keep pushing and eventually, he'll get his way. If he yells at her because he doesn't like the meal she has prepared, his bad temper and rude response are *his* responsibility. If they're talking while he's driving and he misses an exit, then screams at her that it's all her fault, she must realise that *he* is the one driving. Therefore, it is *his* responsibility that he missed the exit.

Warning: If you are seeing these kinds of behaviours in your relationship, it is possible that the situation could become physically dangerous for you. Although some people never cross

that line, these are typical precursors to assault, and escalation soon follows with serious injury or death as potential outcomes.

Seek the advice of a professional who can help you determine what level of risk is involved and what your next steps should be.

Whether you're dealing with substance abuse and other addictions, or any other behaviour that is not conducive to a harmonious relationship or home, the principles are the same. It all comes down to having clear boundaries.

One of the easiest ways to understand what it means to have good boundaries is to remember that what other people say and do is *their* choice. You have no control over what they say or what they do, and no one has that control over you either. You *always* choose your actions, your words and your responses. If you choose to do what someone else wants, needs, demands or expects of you, it's *your* choice.

You might want to blame that person for your choice - "He made me do it!" But the truth is, *you* chose to do it. You could have refused. No one picked up your arms and legs and made your body move like a puppet, no one manipulated your mouth and larynx to make you speak. You could have responded differently. You did not have to get angry when he called you a rotten name and tried to provoke you. When his behaviour was way out of line and he hit you or insulted you, you didn't have to give up your power by feeling like a victim.

Every single thing you say and do is *your* choice, and it's the same for everyone else on the planet. You may have been trained to believe that another person's words or actions are your responsibility, your fault, or under your control, but not everything we believe is the truth. Hidden in plain sight, right in the middle of "belief" is the word, "lie". You may have been trained to believe that you must give up your own thoughts, needs and feelings for others, but that is false. You get to choose. If you want to give up your own needs, that's one thing - and that's fine. But if you feel like you're doing it because of what someone else wants, remember that it's still up to *you*.

Knowing what you need and how you feel, and honouring those needs and feelings by speaking your truth is what it is to have good boundaries. Respecting yourself in this way is what empowers you. It puts you in the driver's seat, where you know you're in control of yourself and your life - and that's the first step to finding fulfillment and happiness.

Invitation: Look at the areas of your life that you would like to change. In particular, do you blame others for your current situation? Forget them for a moment, and look at your own role and all the places in which you made decisions to give up your power, or you made a self-destructive choice, or you trusted someone who betrayed you.

Write about the choices you made so you can see the role you played in ending up where you are right now. I know this might feel a bit daunting and you might still want to blame. But I can promise you that if you are willing to take full responsibility for the choices you've made that contributed to where you are right now, you will become more empowered than ever before. This will be a giant step toward taking control of your life and creating a better future.

An important step in this process is to fully forgive yourself for all the choices you made that didn't do you any favours. Understand that you did your best with whatever circumstances you had at those times, and just let go of your guilt, remorse, and regret. Perhaps burn your list.

Once you've accepted responsibility for where you are, and you've forgiven yourself for your missteps and have let them go, then you can truly move forward and approach your life and choices from a much more empowered place.

Day 17 - To b'lieve, or not to b'lieve. That is the question!

What do you believe? Yeah, I know, that's a huge question because I didn't ask what do you believe about something in particular.

What do you believe in general? What have you been taught throughout your life? About yourself? About what you can expect out of life? About how other people see you, what they expect from you, about your place in the world...about anything and everything?

Yup. Still a big question. But well worth considering.

Okay, here's another one, maybe not quite so broad. Is there anything you'd like to change about yourself or your life? Yeah, I know, the answers to that could be Big Things and they might still be quite broad and general (e.g. "I want to be happy"). But at least a big answer is still an answer and it gives you a starting point if you want to move forward in your life.

Is there any area of your life that feels negative in some way? For example, the way you feel about yourself? Are you one of those people who speak in a self-deprecating way? Do you think you're "not as good as others" or do you think people won't like you, or you wonder why they *do* like you?

Or are you doing things you don't want to be doing but feel like you have no choice because it's just what you've always done or what you think you're supposed to do or what people expect from you?

Basically, are there areas of your life that don't make you happy or that don't work for you in some way?

If the answer to that is "yes," then let me ask you this: Do you want to change any of it? If the answer is "yes" again, start by looking at what you believe about the current situation. I would suggest you write it down. There's a lot of power in seeing the words in front of you, rather than just thinking them in your head. Trust me. This is an important, powerful and empowering step.

Now look at your beliefs. Where did they come from? Did they come from your parents, or others who taught you to have those beliefs? Did they come from some experience(s) in your life? And most importantly, is there any *evidence* to support your beliefs?

It is true that much of what we believe comes from childhood, what we were taught by parents, teachers, other people, or from our life experiences. We go out into the world and act on those beliefs, whether or not they are truth, whether or not they're based in fact. We don't usually stop to question them. We just keep putting one foot in front of the other, making choices based on our beliefs. If we think of them at all, we think of them as fact. ***And we validate those beliefs by continually putting ourselves in positions that match them.***

It is of the utmost importance to understand that a belief is not a fact. It is merely an opinion that is held to be true, which is something else entirely. Opinions and ideas are not facts.

For example, if you're raised in an abusive and oppressive environment, you grow up thinking this is normal. You don't even know it's abusive - it's just the way life is. You believe it's supposed to be like that. So you will surround yourself with people and situations that validate those beliefs.

If you grow up in a home where there is respect and kindness, and where there is nothing that looks like abuse, you believe that's how life should be, and how people should treat each other. That is normal for you, and you will gravitate toward similar situations.

Your experiences shape your beliefs, but you are always free to change what you believe. "The sky is blue, the grass is green", those are facts and cannot be changed. "Everyone is insulted or hit, and that's normal" - that is a belief and I can assure you, it ***can*** - and ***should*** - be changed.

Look at what you want to change. Pick apart your beliefs about those situations. Ascertain which ones are based in facts and which ones are based on your opinions, or the opinions of others. If you hold self-destructive beliefs - that is, any beliefs that harm you or cause you pain or distress, whatever their source - you're free to change them.

If you think you have plenty of evidence to support the validity of self-destructive beliefs (e.g. "I'm a failure. I can't do anything right."), I would challenge you to look for evidence to the contrary and I'm sure you'll find plenty. You'll find many ways in which you've been successful, areas of your life where you've done wonderful things for yourself or others. If you can't find any, ask people you trust to point out where they think you've been successful.

Even if you have failed at something in your life, this does not mean you are "a failure." Your behaviours and experiences are not you. Negative self-talk is based on a subjective opinion that came from you or others. Just because someone else says you are worthless or you're stupid, it does not mean it is a fact. Rest assured that you do not deserve to be insulted.

Everyone makes mistakes. We are all doing our best. We are human; we get it wrong sometimes. But there is a perfect Spirit inside you, flawless and beautiful. You should not be dwelling on - or believing - the hurtful words of someone who insults you, no matter what that person's role is in your life.

You know that deliciously wonderful feeling of having de-cluttered your home? You know, going through the closets, the drawers, the shelves, cleaning out stuff, getting rid of junk, bits that are falling apart, you lost half of that, these don't work any more, are taking up space, you don't need them and forgot you had them etc.?

Rummage around in your brain. Go through its closets and drawers. Haul out the beliefs that you'll find stashed away. Get rid of the junk, the old stuff that doesn't work or you don't need. You'll find plenty of beliefs that are oppressive, inaccurate, or just plain false, and that don't serve any purpose except to cause you harm, to hold you back, to prevent your happiness.

You're free to chuck them. You get to keep the ones you like, the ones that make you happy, that allow you forward movement in your life. And you're allowed to create a bunch of new ones that will add to that. But you don't have to keep the ones that are causing you to stay stuck and unhappy.

They're only thoughts in your head. That means you have complete control over them. Keep them; chuck them. It's up to you. But just bear in mind that the ones you keep are the ones that form the basis for your choices in life. What you believe becomes how you live.

Remember this: Unless and until you change your beliefs, you will continue to surround yourself with situations that validate them - no matter how harmful they are to you, no matter how unhappy they make you.

Choose your beliefs wisely.

Invitation: Go through the above text and find all the places where I asked questions or suggested you write your responses and thoughts. Whenever my students do this powerful exercise as homework in the courses I teach, they find it to be eye-opening, life-changing, and empowering.

Day 18 - …Like Hand In Glove… Or Acid?

Tea and milk. Milk and cookies. Milk and honey. Honey and peanut butter. Peanut butter and strawberry jam. Chicken and strawberry jam. Strawberries and cream. Strawberries and chocolate. Dark chocolate and red wine. Wine and cheese. Wine and picnic baskets. Yogi and picnic baskets.

Afternoon and naps. Naps and kitties. Laps and kitties. Laps and kiddies. Kiddies and cuddles. Cuddles and loved ones. Loved ones and hugs. Hugs and trees. Trees and birds. Singing birds and sunny days. Sunny days and Spain. Spain and olives. Olives and Italy. Italy and passion. Italy and romance.

Good friends and laughter. Good friends and comfort. Comfort and thick duvet. Thick duvet and warm bed. Warm bed and flannel jammies. Warm bed and hot bath. Hot bubble bath and candlelight. Candlelight and soft music. Soft music and sleeping children. Sleeping children and melting heart.

Myriad wonderful pairings in the world… pairings that just go together so naturally, so beautifully, you can't imagine that each part was created separately. (And yes, chicken and strawberry jam is fab in a sandwich… don't knock it till you've tried it!)

If the pairings in your life are milk and poison, or sunny days and road kill, you cannot fully experience or appreciate the beauty that exists around you, in your life, or in yourself.

You and deserving good things. You and being happy. You and feeling peaceful. You and being protected. You and staying safe. You and being shown compassion. You and being nurtured. You and being healed. You and being understood. You and keeping your power. You and feeling joy. You and being creative. You and having freedom. You and self-expression.

These are the kinds of pairings that are perfection itself. These are the kinds of pairings that will allow you to live a beautiful life and experience the very best it has to offer.

Invitation: When a situation or a person presents you with milk and poison, you don't have to drink it. You have the power and the ability to walk away from it and have your milk and honey.

And if you discover that you're the one serving up the poison yourself, as soon as you notice the skull and crossbones on the label of that bottle you're passing around, you can stop, apologise for it, then safely dispose of it where it won't hurt anyone else.

If life is turning your sunny days into one long trail of road kill, check who's behind the wheel. Who – or what – is causing the problem? Is it a mechanical error in the steering? Is it poor judgment or too much speed?

Or is there someone else behind the wheel, taking control while you're covering your eyes and becoming increasingly queasy with every *thump!* as some other little critter gets splattered beneath you?

If you're always busy checking labels for poison, if you're too busy avoiding all the little bunnies and foxes and gophers on the road, how are you going to enjoy the scenery or the sunny day? How will you remember some of the very best pairings, like you and your divinity? You and your Spirit?

To dwell in a toxic environment of negativity and oppression will suffocate every part of your life with thick, dark sludge. If you're choking on negative thoughts and self-destructive actions, if you're allowing negative forces, people, situations in your environment, you're paying for it with your physical, mental and emotional health. You're paying for it with a piece of your soul every day.

In order to enjoy the beauty of your life, you must first welcome, accept and live in positive energy, a positive and thriving environment that is nurturing, gentle, and kind, an environment that allows freedom, love and respect. It's what you deserve – and if you don't believe this, then you're feeding yourself the milk and poison. Perhaps it's time to safely dispose of that nasty little bottle and find the honey instead.

In your thoughts, words, companions, what you read, what you watch, how you behave toward yourself and others...in all aspects of your life, which do you choose?

Day 19 - Worry Is A Prayer for the Negative

Do you worry a lot? That used to be me. I came by it honestly enough. I grew up in a hostile environment and was constantly fearful and anxious, waiting for the other shoe to drop, or for a grand piano to fall on my head. Sure enough, the shoes and pianos kept dropping. So I continued to worry. A lot.

As a kid, I didn't have much choice about what was happening in my environment. I grew up not knowing any different. I'd got so used to worrying and being in fearful situations that I just went from one to the next to the next. It was all I expected from life. I thought I had no choice, no control about any of it. I used to say that if it weren't for bad luck, I wouldn't have any luck at all. And of course, the miseries continued to come. And so did the worry about more.

Eventually, I learned that if you focus on what you want, you'll improve your chances of getting it. If you focus on what you don't want, you'll be more inclined to get that, too.

Let's say you've decided to look for a particular type of job. You're all excited about it. You're thinking about this job a lot, you're imagining yourself in that role and you can't wait to make it happen.

In that frame of mind, you'll be open to spotting an advert about just such a job, or one that sounds like it might be the right one. Or you'll overhear a conversation about it. Or if someone comes to you and says, "I heard about this job possibility for you," you'll jump at the chance and get details and contact information.

On the other hand, if you think you'll be stuck in your job forever, you couldn't possibly change, no one else would hire you anyway, you'd never get any other job, you can't learn anything new or some other bunch of blah blah blah, your eyes will skate right past those adverts. When you overhear a conversation about a job you might like, or someone tells you about a position that sounds just perfect, you'll think, "What's the point, they won't hire me anyway."

You will validate whatever you believe. It's what we do. It's human nature. Your feet will lead you to whatever is on your mind. It's kind of like when you're driving and you go into a skid.

You must ***not*** look where the car is heading or you'll keep steering in that direction. You must look away from the direction of the skid, and instead look back to the safe part of the road where you want to be.

There's a reason for that: You will always follow your gaze, literally and figuratively.

Invitation: If you are inclined to worry, write a list of current worries. Write about whether or not worrying is making you feel better. Is it making you feel more hopeful or positive? Is it benefiting you in any way? Write the worrying thoughts you have, and how they make you feel, including in your physical body. Then write a list of previous worries you had that never actually happened. And write about how much better those periods of time might have been if you had allowed yourself to let go of the worries.

Worry is just a prayer for the negative. So it's like that the more you worry, the worse you feel. And you probably drag a whole lot of whatever you are worrying about right smack into the middle of your life because you are open to it, you are thinking about it, you are focusing on the direction of the skid. So you slam right into the wall or the oncoming vehicle.

Write about the positive ways in which your life would be improved if you let go of your worries.

Whatever "stuff" you've got going on, you don't **have to** worry about it or you're just praying for more of the same. Look away from the skid - turn your attention to where you want your car to be headed - and get back to the safe part of the road.

Day 20 - Yummy Wine or Turpentine?

I wish I had a buck for every time people said that they wished they were as positive as I am. It's kind of funny when I think about it because I can assure you I didn't come out of the chute this way. I've been to hell and back more times than I'd care to think about and because of that, I've finally got to the point of understanding how important it is to focus on the good, the positives, the successes, the happiness, and what I want - and I can let go of thinking about the fears, the failures, and what might (or did) go wrong.

I used to be known as probably the biggest pessimist on the planet. I always said, "If it weren't for bad luck, I wouldn't have any luck at all!" People always said I was so negative, so pessimistic, always expecting the worst etc. And my response was, "Well, the worst always happens so what else do you expect me to do?"

Then I read about an organisation in America called BLOOP - the Benevolent and Loyal Order Of Pessimists. They claimed that contrary to popular belief, they were not gloomy and depressed because 95% of the time they were proven to be right, and 5% of the time they were pleasantly surprised.

On the other hand, they said, 95% of the time optimists were disappointed, and 5% of the time, they were proven to be right. Therefore, optimists couldn't possibly be nearly as happy as pessimists, or so BLOOP members claimed.

I was only too happy to adopt their beliefs as my own. It was a great reason (um, excuse) to continue to expect the worst.

Over the many years since then, I have come to believe that you get what you expect (the majority of the time). So of course, as I look back on a few decades of misery, I can see that I was expecting the worst and it kept happening. I continued to put - or keep - myself in situations and beliefs that would perpetuate it.

Now I expect good things and more than ever before, they're happening. This doesn't mean that my life is perfect or that there aren't challenges. But how I view those challenges is what makes a big difference. And I continue to give as little attention as possible to thinking about them in a negative way.

Instead, I insist on focusing on positives, on health, wellbeing, growth and learning. I'm all about happiness and changing my thoughts to reflect what I want, and not what I don't want, or what I fear. The more I focus on what I want, the less I can even begin to consider what I don't want.

My life is so much lighter and happier for it. And yours can be, too. Every time I'm told how much people wish they could be as positive as I am, or how they wish they could think like I do, I remind them that I wasn't always like this and I know what it is to learn to change those negatives into positives.

Invitation: Once you start focusing on the positives, it will feel so good you'll want to do it more. It gets easier with time; it's just about developing the habit of choosing positive thoughts over negative ones. Doing it is its own reward because it just feels so good to live in a positive frame of mind. Then, when Life lobs a bunch of lemons, it's much easier to get out of the misery and back into a place that feels good.

List some issues about which you are now deciding to be positive, and write how this will impact your life. Once you get good at it, there's no decision to be made. It's like being used to drinking cheap wine and you don't really like it but you're used to it.

Then you start drinking better wine, and soon you discover that the cheap stuff is ***really*** nasty. It doesn't take long and you're bypassing the cheap stuff without even thinking about it, and heading straight for the wine that you enjoy. You will never find yourself standing in front of shelves of wine and asking yourself, "Hmm, should I buy this yummy one that I love? Or this really nasty stuff that's made from turpentine?" The thought would never cross your mind.

You get to choose. Do you want the yummy wine? Then have it.

Learning to trade in your negative thoughts and patterns for positive ones is like getting used to the finest wine. You can never go back to the cheap stuff!

Day 21 - A Second Chance. A Clean slate. A Fresh Start.

Have you ever wished for these? Chances are, you have. I know *I* certainly have...

I've wished I could have a clean slate when I didn't think it was possible. And I've had to start over many times when it was the last thing I wanted. I've messed things up and wished I could take back my mistakes, erase them, wipe away any memory of them that might remain in my own head and especially in the minds of others.

I've been stuck in some utterly horrible situations, feeling trapped, thinking there was no way out. And among the worst were the situations in which my own thoughts were holding me hostage and all I really wanted was to escape and leave them all behind. But I was haunted, my memories unrelenting and unforgiving, no clean slate in sight.

There have been a few times in my life when I've been forced to face the need for a major overhaul, a time out, a serious de-cluttering in my life. When a fresh start was my only hope for redemption.

There are times when no matter how hard you try or how much you wish you could undo something, it's just not possible. The fresh start doesn't take it away. The clean slate still bears a quiet smudge. The second chance cannot become the first, which is still there, lurking in the shadows and taunting you with how you blew it, every chance it gets.

The good news is that if you really want a fresh start or that clean slate, you must remember this: Every day, you're writing your history. Every day, you're creating your story, the story that is your life, the one that becomes your past, the one people will tell about you, and will be handed down for many years to come.

Every moment, every decision, every little choice moves you further away from those disasters that are better left in the past - or closer to more of the same. Whichever you choose.

Any time you want a fresh start or a clean slate, you can create one. Because every moment is a chance to reset your intentions, to check your thinking, to take stock of your current situation, your attitudes, your dcsircs.

Every moment is a new opportunity to refocus your attention on the direction you choose for your life.

No matter how much you mess things up, no matter how many mistakes you make, no matter how much you may have blown it. Every moment is a chance to begin again.

Invitation: Write about any ways in which you would love a fresh start right now, a chance to begin again. Write about how your life would be different because of it in six months, a year, five year - or whatever other timelines you choose.

Then look at each of the items on your list and write about what you can differently so you will ultimately achieve your goal. Some of them might involve longer-term goals that wouldn't let you see results for quite some time. In order to feel encouraged, build confidence and stay on track, break down the long-term goals into some smaller chunks to give yourself an opportunity to see some progress.

Be sure to have some much shorter-term goals, too. As you accomplish simpler ones that allow you to see results fairly quickly, you'll feel motivated to tackle the longer-term ones.

Day 22 - Stop Letting Fear Make Your Decisions!

If you want to make a good decision and have a good result, do not let fear influence you.

I'm not talking about the sensible kind of fear, the instinctive fear that is designed to protect you, like fear of vicious animals, fear of fire, fear of standing at the edge of the roof of a 100-storey building with no guardrail... I'm talking about the really pointless kind. The kind that involves shooting yourself in the foot - totally blasting it to smithereens, and with a 12-gauge shotgun, no less.

Many years ago, I found myself in yet another Major Disaster. A seriously prize-winning, grand scale, "Good grief, I can't believe I managed to do this *again*" sort of mess. Stubborn, single-minded, ruled by my heart and not letting my head get its couple of pennies' worth in - until it was far too late - I didn't listen to the gnawing little voice inside that had tried to warn me.

In fact, I'd got quite good at ignoring it down the years. A massively powerful and painful lesson all by itself, that one...

Anyway, just how had I wound up in another impossibly challenging situation after all I'd learned already?

Feeling defeated, disheartened and discouraged, I had to wonder: Was this my fate? Was it my destiny to work so hard to make the right choices, to have a better life, only to wind up suffering in the same miserable place over and over again?

But wait a minute! What about free will? Didn't that figure in here somewhere, too? I couldn't believe my destiny would be about having to suffer. It occurred to me that I'd been misunderstanding 'destiny'. In that moment, I realised that my destiny is not what I make of my life. It's the *potential* for what I *could* make of it. And I could use my free will to fulfill it - or not.

Okay, so why had I been working so hard for so many years to make the right choices, only to keep finding out that they were the wrong ones? Why did I keep thinking I'd made progress, only to discover that I hadn't, after all?

Eager to find an answer, I spent a couple of days at my computer, writing. I started looking at all the big decisions I'd made since leaving home at 16 years old. I analysed every one of them, and working my way backward through my thought processes in each to discover the roots that led to such disastrous results.

What I learned from those two emotionally challenging and exhausting days changed the course of my life in ways that now astonish me. Every single one of those decisions had been rooted in fear. Fear of being abandoned. Fear of not being loved. So where did all that fear originate? The short answer is that it was rooted in my childhood - and it went right back to my conception, when I feared for my very survival because of the circumstances in my birth mother's life.

As I contemplated the early fearful months and years of my existence, it became crystal clear to me that I had been letting those fears make my decisions for me throughout my life. And then I understood that basing my decisions on fear had never resulted in a good outcome.

I can't begin to tell you what a huge relief it was to reach these conclusions, to put the pieces of my life together in a way that I knew was going to change it for the better. In a way I'd never done before, I was beginning to understand the insanity that had been my life.

Immediately, I knew what I had to do. I made a solemn vow to myself that I would never again let Fear influence my decisions. I was going to stop letting Fear stop ME.

Just days later, I was met with my first challenge. A friend suggested I visit her in England. I'd never really travelled and had some anxiety about going too far from home, residual stuff from being agoraphobic many years earlier. In a heartbeat, loads of nameless fears popped into my head. You'd think the universe might have been nice and given me a small starter challenge or two, just to ease me into this brave new world I'd created for myself.

But nope, I was thrown in headfirst at the deep end of the pool. And I'd got no idea how to swim.

I was a serious homebody. I was terrified. Of what, I didn't know. *Could I go to England? Oh, no, I couldn't. I'm sure I can't afford that, and I've got no one to look after my children* (the three youngest still lived at home). Great reasons. But if I wasn't even going to contemplate finding solutions to these problems, they were really just excuses. *You big chicken.*

Look, I said to myself, *are you going to honour that vow you made to yourself or not? Are you going to cave with the very first time you're confronted with some nameless fears? Aren't you even going to **try** not to let them stop you? Are you going down without even thinking about a fight? I'm so disappointed in you!!!*

Well, that did it. I've always hated disappointing anyone. It was time I realised that I deserved the same respect as I gave everyone else, and stopped disappointing myself, too. I sorted out child care. And an inexpensive charter flight. I sorted out staying with a few friends most of the three weeks I'd be in the UK, and found some inexpensive B & Bs for the rest. Suddenly, I began to look forward to my trip. I still had moments of nervousness, but they were being eaten up by my excitement as my departure date grew closer.

From the moment I landed at Heathrow, and throughout my three glorious weeks in England and Scotland, I was met with countless situations that made me think, "Oh, no! I'm afraid to..." (try this, eat those, go here, do that, blah blah blah).

But I was on a mission. Not just for that journey, but for the rest of my life. If a sentence began with "I'm afraid to..." I had to do whatever it was. And I can honestly say, I'd never felt so exhilarated, never had so much fun, never felt such a growing sense of confidence, freedom and empowerment as I did with every one of those fears that I knocked aside - only to discover there was nothing to have feared in the first place. I was so very grateful to have made that one simple, yet monumental decision - to stop letting fear stop me.

I could write for days about how that one decision changed my life. But the first and most obvious to anyone who has known me since I lived in Canada is that I ended up moving to England 10 months after that first trip, and you'll know just how much my life and I changed as a result of it.

I began writing books. Started painting and within weeks was selling my work, had pieces in a couple of galleries, and soon was invited to have a solo exhibition. My abilities as a psychic and medium, which had gradually evolved over the years, suddenly blossomed. I was tearing all over the UK and the rest of Europe having a blast.

The whole world opened up to me because I'd opened myself up to the world. Opportunities and possibilities were everywhere and I was leaping on loads of them, changing my life for the better in more ways than I could tell you.

And none of it would have happened if I'd stayed in Calgary, fearful of nameless, silly things that would have kept me trapped and suffocating in the fearful little box that was my life. I had no idea what there was 'out here', outside the fearful little box.

The world - and my life - just keep expanding, making me want to see more, do more, be more. And all because of that one decision to stop letting fear stop me...

Invitation: Write about as many of your big decisions as you want. Peel them back a layer at a time and see how many of them were based on fear. Write about the outcomes and how your life might have been easier or better or different if you hadn't let fear make those decisions for you. Go deep. Let this one really sink into your being. Allow yourself to see the possibilities if you stop letting fear stop you. This is one of the most powerful, positively life-altering exercises you will ever do.

Day 23 - When Fear Masquerades as Love

It is said that everything we think and do comes from one of two emotions: love or fear. I used to dispute this. I figured it was rubbish. But in the many years since first hearing that, I've been putting this theory to the test and I have to admit, it is the truth. When I take an honest look at my words, my reactions, and my choices, everything is rooted in one of these two emotions.

This can get a bit tricky sometimes, though. There have been occasions when I thought I was doing something out of love. I love this person; therefore I am doing this loving thing, both of which may be quite true. But then how could it turn out to be something harmful to me or destructive in some way? Can anything motivated by love actually be hurtful?

Well...yes and no. The "no" is the easiest bit. In and of itself, love is not harmful or destructive. "Yes" if there is fear connected to it in some way - because the bottom line is that a choice that is ultimately destructive will still have been rooted in fear.

For example, there is a big difference between "I need you because I love you", and "I love you because I need you." In a romantic relationship, it should be the former, but unfortunately, it is very often the latter, which is quite destructive.

When we are living in the latter situation, the "love" is driven by need. And the need is driven by fear, for example a fear of being rejected, abandoned, alone, or unloved. In those cases, needful attachment, infatuation and desperation are often disguised as "love."

Therefore, although our actions may have a loving intent on the surface, they have really come from fear on an even deeper level. "I'll do this for you because I love you and I'm terrified that you're going to leave me, or stop loving me" (or whatever).

You may genuinely love someone, for all he or she is - or isn't. Even if that person is disrespectful to you, abusing you, or taking advantage of you. Love, in that case, is certainly not doing you much good on a personal level. And chances are, if you look beneath the surface, you will still find fear lurking there, fear that allows you to tolerate such behaviour out of insecurity, feelings of unworthiness or low self-esteem.

When you allow yourself to examine your fears and perhaps discover what may have caused them, you can also allow yourself to heal them. And sometimes, even if you still carry the fear, you don't have to let it make your choices. It's okay to feel fear, as long as you don't let it stop you or be the reason for a decision that will ultimately hurt you.

You may be thinking, "But wait a minute! Sometimes people do things out of anger or hurt or jealousy!" Yes, that's true. But if you peel back where those emotions come from, they will all be rooted in fear. For example, if you are jealous about a woman at the office who keeps eyeing your husband, it is because you fear losing him. Greed may stem from a fear of poverty, or of being seen as inadequate or unsuccessful. And how many parents do you know who are furious with their children for having gone missing or for doing something dangerous? Their anger is borne out of a fear of something awful happening to their children.

I'm not suggesting there's anything wrong with feeling fear. Nor am I suggesting that you should live in a constant state of peace and joy, or never having a scary thought or a worry enter your head, let alone allow it to settle in your soul for any length of time.

You are still human; you can't avoid feeling fear sometimes. It's what you do with it that matters.

Learn to recognise its hateful and ugly little spirit. Sometimes it disguises itself and pretends to be a genuine concern for someone, or a worry about a situation. Occasionally, it masquerades as a supposedly legitimate consideration of a potentially unpleasant outcome if a particular course of action is taken.

But as intelligent and rational as these seem to be, and as much sense as they seem to make at the time, they are still based in fear and if you were to make a decision in that frame of mind, it would not yield a positive result in the long run.

When you can see through every brilliant facade that is manufactured by Fear, and you're well acquainted with the damage it can do, you will respect how nasty it can be if you let it infiltrate your life and your choices. Decide right now that you will refuse to give it any such power or pleasure again and stand by that decision, no matter what. I can promise you, it will change your life for the better.

When you can do this, then you can see quite clearly if your choices are merely Fear disguised as Love, or whether they're the real thing. In all difficult moments, difficult interactions, frustrating and painful situations or stressful times, if you repeatedly - and honestly - check your motivation as you move through them, the best result will always - and only - come from Love.

Invitation: Write about some of your most challenging relationships, events, incidents, moments or experiences. Be completely, painfully honest with yourself. Dig down to the roots of why you felt or behaved as you did. Look at what motivated you in your choices.

Write about the consequences of your choices. How did they impact you? Others? Situations? Use this opportunity to become more self-aware than you've ever been.

Fear can masquerade as Love. But Love has nothing to do with Fear.

Day 24 - Your Well-Being Is Your Greatest Asset

No one can take care of you except *you*. It's your job, your responsibility. You'll be no good to yourself or anyone else if you let yourself decline into a state of ill health, whether physically, mentally, emotionally or spiritually.

And if you don't value and respect yourself enough to take care of your health and your well-being on all levels, how can you expect anyone else to value and respect you?

When I was a counsellor many years ago, and later as a homeopath, I used to hear parents tell me that they had low self-esteem, or none at all.

At some point, we would discuss their children's self-esteem and the parents always said they were teaching their children to love themselves and have a good self-image and sense of self-worth.

I would ask, "Can you play the tuba?"

Invariably, they would say, "No."

I'd suggest, "Then I want you to teach your children how to play it."

Of course, they were puzzled and always stared at me in confusion.

I would tell them, "How are you going to teach your children to have a good sense of self-esteem if yours is low or non-existent?"

There is only one *you*. You're irreplaceable and a divinely perfect spirit residing in a body that needs care and attention. Safeguard all aspects of yourself and your well-being.

Model this love and appreciation for yourself and your well-being so that others will look up to you and want to emulate your healthy actions.

Take care of the most valuable asset you have: Yourself - in mind, body and spirit. You deserve it. And the rest of us are counting on you being well and lighting up your corner of the world as only you can do.

Invitation: Write about the ways in which you have been neglecting yourself. Add all areas of life including socially, hobbies, etc. Then write about all the ways in which you're going to change that and make sure that every single day, you take steps to include self-care into your life. Every evening, jot down a list of "how you did" to help keep you focused.

Day 25 - That Little Voice Inside Never Lies...

You know that little voice inside? The one that seems to come from your guts when something just doesn't sit right? The one that is so easy to ignore? How many times have you kicked yourself for not having listened to it? How many times have you discovered, much to your chagrin, that it had been right? If you're like most people (myself included), the answer is "many."

And how many times have you discovered that it was wrong? I would suggest that if you're completely honest with yourself, the answer is "never."

I'm not talking about the little voice that tells you other people will be disappointed if you don't do what they want, or the one that worries about what other people think. That little voice is your Ego, your fearful human self and it all too often it has the best interests of other people at heart.

I'm talking about the little voice that has *your* best interests at heart. The one that knows what is really best for you. The one that warns you of situations that just don't feel right, saying, "This isn't good for you!"

That little voice is your Highest Self. Calling itself "intuition", it is your Spirit connecting with you, speaking to you with the purest wisdom. Learning to trust it is one of our most difficult lessons. Sometimes we ignore it because although we know it's right, we want to please someone or we're afraid to stand up for ourselves.

Sometimes we find ourselves wanting to do something but that little voice says it's wrong, it's bad for us or it's self-destructive or self-sabotaging. But we want to do it anyway (whatever "it" is) because it's fun or sinful or delicious or exciting or naughty so we refuse to heed the wisdom of those quiet little words.

The regret may happen immediately; it may take some time. But at some point, we will end up acknowledging - if only to ourselves - that we should have listened. At some point, we recognise that there were consequences for ignoring that little voice.

Maybe minor ones that aren't such a big deal in the grand scheme of things, or maybe massive ones that have had a profoundly negative, life-altering impact. And despite all of that, sometimes we will continue as before, still not heeding the wisdom of that quiet little voice.

I'm sure you know exactly what I'm talking about.

As human beings, with consciousness and intelligence, we think we know best. We think we have the greatest wisdom. We are capable of great accomplishments and achievements. We invent and create. We build whole cities. We put men on the moon.

But in our arrogance, as human beings we don't realise that consciousness and intelligence only give the illusion of incredible greatness and wisdom.

It is said that we are not human beings having a spiritual experience; we are spiritual beings having a human experience. Your purpose is to connect with your Spirit so you can learn from it. In doing so, you will see who you could become if you maintained that connection. To live in a state of constant communication with your Spirit, or your Highest Self, is to be truly enlightened and living a purely authentic life.

All that building and creating that we do in our humanness serves many purposes, one of which is to enable us to survive. But the greatest building and creating come from the omnipotent wisdom of the Spirit. Human existence would be cold, empty and meaningless without the forgiveness, the compassion, the warmth and the love that come from connecting with the Divine Spirit that lies within each of us.

This is the challenge for us. Every day, we're bombarded by the struggles of Life that test us, giving us opportunities to grow, to learn, to become more connected with our Highest Selves. We are confronted with anger and indignation, frustration and jealousy, grief and loneliness. We are challenged in our relationships with others, and with ourselves. Everywhere we look, our humanness stares us in the face, tempting us to resist change, take the easy way out and simply slide into those familiar but painful responses and patterns.

The challenge for us is to look past our humanness, connect with our Spirits, find the lessons it wants to teach us, and learn them. If you listen for it, you'll hear that little voice. And the more you communicate with your Spirit, the easier it becomes. Just as you know the result of ignoring it, I'm sure you also know the joy and the strength that come from listening to it and taking its advice.

No doubt that on many occasions in which it's done battle with your humanness, it will have won. You've done the right thing. The pure thing. The good thing. The thing that allows you to grow, to become empowered, or to be more connected with your Spirit, your Highest Self.

It's okay if you falter on this journey now and then. It's okay if you take one step forward and two steps backward sometimes. That's the human experience of a spiritual being. The challenge is to continue taking steps forward, doing your best to learn from the places that trip you up.

It begins with listening to that little voice inside. It is the source of the greatest strength, the greatest intelligence, and the greatest wisdom in the Universe. It knows the truth - always - even when you don't want to know it. It will always guide you in the direction of the highest good. It will always lead you closer to spiritual perfection and Enlightenment.

If all of us walk on this path, we will become more at peace with ourselves and with each other. It may not always be easy. It may not be easy at all. But it will be very well worth it.

<u>Invitation</u>: Write about those times that you ignored that little voice. Write about why you chose to do that, and what the outcome was.

Bear in mind, we're not talking about the little voice that is about what other people think. We're talking about the one that gives advice that you really know you ought to take but you chose not to listen and suffered the consequences later.

You might like to write a conversation with your little voice. Talk to it - in writing. And write the responses you get. It's a good way to begin to connect with your Highest Self. Ask what it wants you to know. Ask about specific concerns or problems you've got right now. Ask what you should do next.

When you are willing to be very still so you can listen to that little voice, and when you're willing to follow its advice, you will begin to see much more positive results for your life.

Day 26 - Avoid "Empty Refrigerator Syndrome"

Are you tired? Exhausted, you say? Wrung out? I know what you mean. There's always something to suck the life and energy out of us, isn't there? Working 47 hours a day on a job you. Maybe it's the demanding boss who knows all too well that he can pile on too much work because you really need that job.

Or perhaps it's the husband who wants dinner on the table at exactly 6 pm and the children should be silent and the house should be spotless and oh, dear, you'd better take off that apron, fix your hair, throw on a little lipstick and look fresh and beautiful when he walks in the house. Or maybe it's the high maintenance wife who can't seem to spend money fast enough in her pursuit of looking like a glamorous movie star on your parts clerk salary.

Then there are the children who need, need, **need** affection and time and homework help and room tidying assistance, or your shoulder for her tears because the object of her crush just humiliated her in front of the whole class, and the family needs dinner and the baby won't stop fussing and refuses to be put down and you got only a few hours' sleep last night and your head is exploding but you have to cook that bloomin' meal anyway and deal with all these children...

And your bank account just looooves the colour red much more than it loves black and it's like you're playing a losing game of checkers with it because it always ends up saying "King me!"

Or the snooty skinny gorgeous (damn her) co-worker who has to whine at you about how her doctor wishes she could gain ten pounds but no matter how many chocolates she eats, or how many pounds of spaghetti, or how much butter is dripping off those countless thick slices of fresh, crusty French bread she eats, she just can't gain an ounce.

Or the mother-in-law who constantly reminds you that you could never be anywhere near as good as the perfect ex-partner of her son or daughter. Or the neighbours who can't wait to tell you their perfect child is on the honour roll, is class president, and in 17 clubs and extra-curricular activities, while your kid is lucky to show up at school with his clothes on right-side-out.

And it's holidays and birthdays and gifts and shopping and decorating and parties and company and *We have to* and *I should* and *It's tradition*, all of which are big bullies and shove aside the whole meaning and purpose of holidays, whether it's Christmas or Pesach or birthdays or just a family visit to Aunt Marsha's in the summer, and it ends up being a miserable, frustrating, depressing and utterly disappointing time.

Yeah, there are lots of reasons to feel exhausted and fed up and you keep trying to hold it all together but despite your best efforts, the house looks more like Roseanne's than Harriet Nelson's, and forget her pearls around your neck, it feels more like there's a noose, and your whole life feels like you're trying to fill a colander with water. Everywhere you look, there are demands and needs and drains on your time, your money, your energy, your patience, and your spirit.

I spent 12 years as a volunteer for the Post-Partum Support Society in Calgary, offering support to women who were struggling with varying degrees of depression after the births of their children. I studied social work, too, during that period, and did some counselling work, and later became a homeopath, listening to a lot of detail about the struggles in my patients' lives.

In all of these situations, whatever specific troubles these people were having, there were many similarities among them. Over and over again, I heard about different versions of the same kinds of problems. One of the toughest and most common ones was the trouble they had in dealing with other people's expectations. We try so hard to be or do what others expect of us, need from us, want from us, that we neglect ourselves, and our own needs.

Whatever you do, whether it's house work or family stuff, or dealing with your sister and her kids or your neighbours who want to rub your nose in their success, or your mother expecting you to be perfect, or your boss who expects the world - you will never please everyone. You will never get it all done. There will always be something left to do, some job or other waiting, some piece of your life that just has to wait.

So let it wait. Put yourself way up at the top of that list of priorities. No one else is gonna do it, so if you want to be in the best possible shape to be able to give and do and help and work and **and** *and* - ad infinitum - then you have to be sure and take care of yourself first in order to be well and fully functional.

So go on. Take a look, see what it is you really need to do so you can get some help or a break whatever will get you feeling energised again. You - and everyone who loves and cares about you - will be much happier for it.

<u>Invitation</u>: Write about the balance - or lack of it - in your life. Think about all the ways in which there is way too much being taken out of your fridge and not much of anything being put back into it.

Find ways that you can cut out some of the extraneous parts - because there will be some, whatever you want to say about it. If you ended up in hospital tomorrow (heaven forbid), the boss, the family, the world would carry on without you for a while.

If you don't set boundaries for yourself, you can't expect anyone else to do it for you. They will keep walking all over you, taking as much as you can possibly give, and not paying any attention to how depleted you are.

Ask for help. Delegate. Increase doses of Vitamin N (i.e. say "No!"). Take stock of what you say are priorities and be realistic about what really has to stay on the list and what can go.

Once you start restocking your own fridge, you'll begin to feel a whole lot better. You'll feel happier, more balanced, and less resentful. You'll have more energy and it will boost your self-esteem and sense of self-worth. It's absolutely essential for you to take care of yourself first. If you don't, you won't be much good to anyone else. You know what they say at the beginning of a flight: Put on your own oxygen mask first!

Just remember this little poem I wrote back in the Dark Ages for those women battling post-partum depression and the many demands of motherhood:

<u>My Advice for Doing Versus Leaving Housework and Other Undesirable Stuff</u>

Do your best and leave the rest,
Tomorrow will soon be today.
And if you're dead by then instead,
It won't matter to you anyway!

- Liberty Forrest (1986)

Day 27 - Move the Cereal Box or Go Somewhere Else

It's human nature to repeat patterns of behaviour, especially when it involves an unresolved emotional issue that's lying there for us to trip over again and again. It's not even a conscious choice. It's like we're on auto-pilot with old recordings playing in our subconscious minds, driving us to try again, fix it this time, make it work, get it right, correct the mistake, and playing not-so-quietly in the background is a constant loop of "Maybe this time, maybe this time, maybe this time."

Whether that unresolved issue has its roots in childhood or a more recent experience, unless and until there is real healing and resolution of it, we continue to play out that original trauma, the original painful incident that has left us wounded or broken. We cannot escape the inherent need to put it right. This is why we keep finding ourselves in the same kinds of situations or facing the same problems again and again. They might wear different clothes, or come in a different shape or size but whatever the mask or disguise might be, what lies underneath is always the same.

And there we are, "in it" yet again.

It's like being one of those tiny plastic wind-up toys that walks. You fish him out of the cereal box, wind him up and set him on the kitchen table. Staring straight ahead, he walks, walks, walks, oblivious to the box in his path until he smacks right into it. His little arms and legs are still moving but he's not going anywhere.

You pick him up, put him back at his "start" position, and he walks, walks, walks - still not seeing the box that is directly in his path - and then he slams into it yet again. Arms and legs still moving, and still not getting anywhere.

As long as you keep him wound up, and you continue to move him back to his "start" position and set him in the same direction, this will happen over and over again. Only when you remove the cereal box, or when you set him down in a new direction will you get a different result.

Invitation: If you're tired of being that little man and you don't want to smack into that cereal box ever again, write about the places in your life where you've continued to repeat the same patterns, make the same unhealthy choices, or respond to situations again and again in ways that just don't serve you well.

What are your triggers? What are the similarities amongst the most challenging situations that keep you smacking into that cereal box? Write about the results you would prefer to see and what it would take to have things turn out that way. What do you need to do differently? How can you avoid smacking into that cereal box again? Embracing your dark side and working toward not letting it adversely impact your life will be one of the best choices you've ever made.

Day 28 - Where Does Self-Worth Originate?

Most of us have stories about the rotten things people have told us about ourselves. Or rather, what they ***believe*** to be the truth about us. It's especially hurtful and damaging when such unkind comments come from our parents when we're just little kids. We're hard-wired to trust our parents; it's an instinct, a necessary survival mechanism built in to protect us.

So we believe every word that comes out of their mouths, or the mouths of other respected family members or dear friends or teachers. Their opinions shape the way we view ourselves and we're only too ready to accept these negative words as the truth, without question, because that's what children do.

We're also hard-wired to live in hunter-gatherer societies, relying on one another for our survival. Therefore, it is human nature to seek approval. Our instincts make us want to fit in and be part of the group so we take on board the judgments and opinions of those with whom we interact throughout our lives.

We're happy to soak up the positive comments, basking in the deliciousness of approval and praise whenever they are offered. Equally, we will also soak up the harsh criticisms and put-downs, taking them to heart at least as easily.

Once we take a few steps down that road, we begin to doubt or reject the positive comments and it becomes increasingly easy to digest the nasty ones. Childhood seeds, long since planted and well rooted, allow us to believe people who say we aren't good enough. Even if it isn't on a conscious level, even if we tell ourselves that's not the truth, somewhere deep inside ourselves we believe those words.

We're talking about your self-worth. What you do, the choices you make, what you believe about your Self (I am writing it that way deliberately) and your place in the world, how you treat others, how you treat your Self - everything about your self-worth comes from your Self. You get to decide what kind of person you are. You get to decide whether or not you have worth and value.

And if you are going to decide you don't, I can assure you that the basis for that decision did not come from your Self. It came from others who planted toxic seeds, which, over the years, you have allowed to be fertilised and fed so they've taken root and twisted their way through your soul.

You did not come out of the chute believing your Self to be rubbish. You entered this world, a blank canvas, a smiling, giggling little baby filled with wonder and ready to be molded and shaped by the events and environments you would experience. You entered the world thinking it revolved around you, another survival instinct to ensure that you got your needs met.

Other people's opinions are just words. When they get into your head, they're still just words. And usually, the hurtful words of another just come from their own feelings of inadequacy and insecurity. There is nothing saying you have to believe the harsh comments that are crammed down your throat by anyone else, no matter who it is, no matter how important that person is to you.

<u>Invitation</u>: You didn't have much choice about what you heard or believed when you were young because you didn't know better. But now, you do. Now you know you have the ability to choose your thoughts, and you can choose to accept or disregard the opinions of other people. Yours is the only opinion that matters when it comes to evaluating your Self and your worth.

If you want to improve your sense of Self-worth, then you are the only one who can make it happen. Write about the unkind thoughts and beliefs you have about yourself and how you came to have them. Dig deep! If you allow yourself to find the roots of destructive beliefs, you can begin working on deleting them and creating healthier, more positive ones.

Day 29 - Remember Your Divinity

I'm going to ask you a question. Please take a moment or two to consider your answer before continuing to read.

Ready? Okay.

When's the last time you hurt yourself?

Please think about that for a moment...

Your answer will depend upon what the question meant to you. Chances are you were wondering when you last stubbed your toe, cut yourself shaving or banged yourself up in some other physical way.

Let's look at some other options that might be more useful. Let's assume for a moment that it was just such an incident. What did you say in that moment? Maybe something like "I'm so stupid!" or "What an idiot!"

Unfortunately, loads of people do make these kinds of statements on a regular basis if they've forgotten something, or made a mistake, mislaid an item - or for other minor infractions. And heaven forbid there should be something more serious!

Do you ever get up in the morning and say, "Hmm, today I think I'll do less than my best!"? Of course you don't. No one makes that decision. Whatever you do, or don't do, you're always doing the best you can do on that day, in whatever circumstances exist at that time, full stop. It's irrelevant whether it's a bad day or a good day or you're tired or upset or it's not the best you have done on other days. It is still the best you can do in that moment, unless you know that you've ever made a conscious decision to do less than your best.

Beating yourself up with unkind comments and negative self-talk will never be helpful, and in fact, such behaviour is quite damaging. Every malignant syllable sinks quietly into your soul, spreading its toxicity and delighting as your sense of self-esteem and self-worth slowly decay.

No doubt you're frequently tearing around doing this and that for other people, keeping yourself very busy with a long list of Things To Do, but neglecting to put your own needs, your own care on that list. You tell yourself "Later, later, later...it's okay, I'm fine," and you keep rushing through your life, head down and gritting your teeth as though you're blindly pushing your way through a Saturday-before-Christmas crowd of shoppers.

It's bad enough to leave yourself off the list. It's worse when you notice your needs and choose to ignore them. You feel exhausted and need extra rest. You don't want to entertain Uncle Henry and Aunt Mildred next Tuesday. You'd rather stay home and put your feet up, than go to that concert for which you bought tickets. You don't feel like cleaning the house today; you'd rather goof off, go hiking, sit in a park, visit a museum, or have a hot soak or a cold beer.

But you know what? If you listen to that call to take some time off, you'll feel so much better for it. You have a duty, an obligation, and a responsibility to take care of yourself and to find balance with work, rest and play. Resting, having fun and enjoying life are not luxuries. They are an essential part of ensuring that you are healthy on all levels.

Isn't it time to stop hurting yourself? Isn't it time to remember your Spirit, which is who you really are? It is pure and perfect; it is your divinity. It does not deserve to be ignored, neglected or insulted. It deserves to be respected, loved, and revered.

In return, your nourished and nurtured Spirit will show you a life that is more beautiful than you could have imagined. The world and its possibilities will open up to you when you are rested, rejuvenated, self-respecting, honouring your Spirit. That is the path to true happiness and inner peace.

Please. Be gentle with yourself. Be kind to yourself. Honour, respect and love yourself. It is what you deserve as the divine and perfect Spirit that you are.

Invitation: Write about the ways in which you hurt yourself. How often do you hurt yourself by ignoring your needs? By not listening to your tired, stressed, and overworked body? By ignoring your out-of-balance life? By not listening to your Spirit screaming for a little "time out" or some meditation, some quiet time to reflect, to play, to draw, to create, to be still, or to laugh?

Living that way is not only destructive on a physical level; it damages your mental, emotional and spiritual well-being, too.

There is much more to life than working to the point of exhaustion and taking care of the physical and material aspects of your existence. Your inner world is just as important as your outer world. In fact, if all is not right on the inside, you're more likely to have everything fall apart on the outside.

Day 30 - How Do You Treat Yourself?

I ended the entry for Day 29 with these words: "Please. Be gentle with yourself. Be kind to yourself. Honour, respect and love yourself. It is what you deserve as the divine and perfect Spirit that you are."

Today I'd like you to take a few moments and look at those words. Sure, they sound like great ideas. And you might take a quick scan and be thinking, "yeah, I do all that stuff", or "I know, I know, I've heard it before and know I should" or "sometimes I do"... but whatever you're thinking, please bear with me for a few moments and let's take a closer look at them.

"Be gentle with yourself." What does that mean? More specifically, what does that mean to you? I can't answer that for you, of course, because I'm not you. But what I hope it means, at the very least, is that you don't place unreasonable demands and expectations on yourself, and especially in times of extra stress or difficulties. I hope you don't beat yourself up for things that are not your responsibility, or for things that you cannot change or control.

I hope you're not eating guilt by the plateful, and washing it down with pitchers of shame, especially as you are always doing the best you can do in whatever circumstances exist at any given moment. I hope it means that on days when you're feeling emotionally battered and bruised, you wrap yourself up in cotton wool, protecting and removing yourself from situations which will only make things worse.

"Be kind to yourself." What does this mean to you? Are you kind to yourself? If so, how? I'm asking you to think about it because sometimes we assume that we're treating ourselves well, but in reality, we are not doing as good a job as we thought.

And if not, why not? Please do reflect on these questions for a moment and answer before you carry on reading.

There is an endless list of ways in which you could be kind to yourself but the most important idea I want to get across to you is not 'how' you do it, just that you do it. Treat yourself to something special - which doesn't have to involve spending money (although it can). It can just mean turning off the phones and watching your favourite show while having a yummy cuppa or glassa something.

And if you're counting calories, like so many people are, it might just mean saying to heck with it now and then and having that 'forbidden delight' that would give you a little pleasure.

It can mean having some compassion for yourself, especially when you're tired or feeling defeated. It can mean seeing yourself as a dejected little kid who could use an arm around his/her shoulders, and telling that little kid that it's gonna be okay, or 'you can do it' or whatever other reassuring words you might need to hear.

It can mean writing or saying affirmations to yourself, giving yourself positive messages each day, nurturing yourself as though you are parenting the little child inside you and wanting that child to feel special and to thrive.

"Honour, respect, and love yourself." On the surface, that may not sound like a tall order. But it is, if you're going to do each of these and do them well.

It shouldn't even be a tall order. In a perfect world, we would all live this way naturally. Unfortunately, because of what we learn from various experiences and influential people, and because of the difficulties that Life throws at us throughout our lives, the resulting damage can leave us behaving dishonourably, disrespectfully and unlovingly toward ourselves - and to others, which is a double whammy, as it is just one more way we're doing it to ourselves, too.

Once again, I would ask you to think about those words: "Honour, respect and love yourself." Contemplate what they mean to you.

These words should mean that you listen to yourself, to what you need, to how you feel. They do not mean that you should always get your way. But they do mean that you should not compromise yourself or your values, especially if you are being coaxed or coerced by someone else. You should not be forced into situations that undermine your morals.

These words should mean that you are at least aware of your needs and feelings, and that you give them equal time and consideration when you're dealing with those of someone else. They should mean that you mind your boundaries, which means knowing very well what is your responsibility and what is someone else's, and that you are assertive and stand up for yourself when necessary.

These words should mean that you understand your value, your worth as the pure and perfect Spirit that you are, and that you behave in alignment with that knowledge, to the best of your ability.

If you hold this vision for yourself and keep it uppermost in your mind, you will find strength and guidance that will help to carry you forward on your journey.

Invitation: Write about the ways in which you have not been honouring, respecting or loving with yourself. Write about why you have made those choices and how you felt for doing it.

Examine some of the most significant events or situations in which you can now see that you weren't honouring yourself. Write about how things might have gone if you had been more loving and respectful of yourself, and how you would have felt about yourself for having done it.

Look at current situations in your life and see where you are not honouring yourself. Write about the ways in which you can be more loving, gentle, and respectful of yourself as you move forward, and consider the benefits for living that way on an ongoing basis.

ABOUT THE AUTHOR

Inspirational speaker Liberty Forrest is an award-winning author and Huffington Post contributor. She has written several books covering a range of self-development, healing and empowering topics.

She is also an artist, specialising in abstract and expressive paintings, as well as in landscape murals.

For about five years, Liberty made frequent guest appearances on BBC Radio doing "psychic phone-ins". She has also worked as a medium on stage, connecting audience members with loved ones in spirit. With a background in social work and counselling, Liberty added an extra element of support and comfort to her readings.

Liberty has enjoyed being a musician since childhood. More recently, she has begun combining her life experience with her love of music, and now composes songs of empowerment and overcoming obstacles.

As a speaker and occasional stand-up comic, Liberty loves to incorporate humour when sharing her inspiring messages of hope and healing.

Visit her websites: www.libertyforrest.com, and www.creativeclaritydesigns.com
Connect on Facebook: facebook.com/libertyspage
Follow on Twitter: @libertyforrest

www.ingramcontent.com/pod-product-compliance
Lightning Source LLC
Chambersburg PA
CBHW060517300426
44112CB00017B/2707